50 Mathematics Lessons

Also available from Continuum

100+ Ideas for Teaching Mathematics – Mike Ollerton

Teaching Mathematics in the Primary School – Gill Bottle

Even Better Mathematics – Afzal Ahmed and Honor Williams

Pocket PAL: Building Learning in Mathematics – Stephanie Prestage, Els De Geest and Anne Watson

That's Maths! (book and CD-ROM) – Tim Harding

50 Mathematics Lessons

Rich and Engaging Ideas for Secondary Mathematics

Colin Foster

continuum

Continuum International Publishing Group

The Tower Building	80 Maiden Lane
11 York Road	Suite 704
London SE1 7NX	New York NY 10038

www.continuumbooks.com

First published 2008
Reprinted 2011

British Library Cataloging-in-Publication Data
A catalogue record for this book is available from the British Library.

ISBN: 9781847061027 (paperback)

Library of Congress Cataloguing-in-Publication Data
Foster, Colin.
    50 mathematics lessons : rich and engaging ideas for secondary mathematics / Colin Foster.
       p. cm.
    Includes bibliographical references.
    ISBN 978-1-84706-102-7
  1. Mathematics--Study and teaching (Secondary)--Activity programs. 2. Lesson planning. I. Title.

    QA11.2.F67 2008
    510.71'2--dc22

                                    2008019541

1007085883
Typeset by Ben Cracknell Studios
Printed and bound in Great Britain

Contents

Introduction

When the occasion demands it, most maths teachers can pull out an all-singing-all-dancing lesson or two that is more or less guaranteed to go well. These can come in handy for job interviews or during inspections. But such lessons tend to require an exceptional amount of preparation or are excessively demanding to deliver and are not sustainable in the real world, where a teacher may have to teach eight or more lessons in a day. For most of us, normal teaching life probably exists nearer the other end of the maths lesson spectrum, with relatively dull, routine and expository lessons, many of which conform to what Jane Annets has called the 'triple-X' model: *explanation*, *examples*, *exercises*. This sort of lesson requires little preparation and is easy to teach, but tends to be uninspiring for learners and unsatisfying for the teacher.

The 50 lessons in this book aim somewhere in between these two extremes: they require only a few minutes of preparation time yet, I hope, rise above the commonplace. I have tried to avoid the predictable, dull and mechanical; yet neither are the ideas intended to be spectacular one-offs. I hope they are better than average, but they are the sort of lessons you could teach eight of in a *day*, rather than eight of in your *career*!

For instance, suppose you wanted to work on the topic of gradient with a Year 7 or 8 group. It would be easy to make up a lesson which involved telling them what gradient is, talking about car journeys over mountains, drawing a few diagrams, and getting the learners working through pages of straightforward questions. You could do that – anyone could do that. But alternatively you could hit the same topic by starting with a scenario that leads learners into examining straight lines and arriving at the idea of steepness for themselves (see Lesson 49: Tricky Triangles). Provided you have the idea, it isn't any harder to make the lesson much more interesting and powerful. And if it takes slightly longer, yet the learners remember it better and understand it more deeply, you won't need to spend so much time revising it later.

For each lesson, I have stated any necessary materials that occur to me. Often there are extra resources available at www.50maths.com. (They are listed there by lesson number and you can just click on what you want – there is no logging-in procedure.) You will find copies of diagrams for printing out or displaying via a projector, and sometimes there are related programs that may be useful either in the classroom or for marking work. There are also some links to other sites.

Within the description of each lesson I have tried to give 'answers' wherever possible. Often it seemed easiest to give an algebraic generalization, but although learners may well arrive at such results I don't mean to imply that 'getting the formula' should necessarily be seen as the desired end-point for any particular learner. Good tasks develop a life of their own and should be readily extendible for learners who need further challenges. I have also indicated on many occasions in a 'Further Ideas' section extra work that might be undertaken by a keen pupil. It is important for the teacher to be aware that often the notional title of the lesson is rather incidental to what the learners will really be working on. (Who cares whether anyone knows what a 'Harshad number' is? See Lesson 18.) Often, what is valuable is the mathematics that is studied *en route*. These lessons are not intended as special end-of-term 'something different' lessons; on the contrary, a lot of Key Stage 3–4 core curriculum topics could be covered very well using the lessons in this book.

It seemed pointless to try to indicate how long these tasks might take – many could well occupy more than one lesson. This is obviously a matter for the judgement of the particular teacher, who is the person who knows the learners and the time constraints. No doubt some ideas will fly and some will flop; I would be very glad of any comments/criticisms. As you read through the lessons, I am not expecting a 'Wow!' reaction. But I hope that at least some of them will appeal to you as interesting and fun ways into important mathematical ideas.

I am very grateful to colleagues for their wisdom but especially to the pupils on whom I have inflicted these lessons, and from whom I'm sure I've learned far more than they have learned from me.

Colin Foster
May 2007

A Prime Example Of A Code

1

Prime numbers have important applications in making and breaking modern-day codes, but the mathematics involved is complex. This task is a different way of constructing a prime number code that is still based on the same mathematical principle of 'unique factorization', the property that if you break up any integer into prime factors, you can do it in only one way (disregarding the order in which you write the factors); e.g., $240 = 2^4 \times 3 \times 5$ only.

The first 26 prime numbers neatly reach to just over 100 (101 is the 26th prime), so it is tempting to identify the letters of the alphabet with these numbers. Learners will need this list – and they can either construct it themselves or be given it (a copy is at www.50maths.com) – see on the right. An advantage of using prime numbers is that the list is not as obvious as, say, the integers 1 to 26 would be, and yet can be constructed by thought alone; it doesn't have to be memorized or carried around, which could make the code vulnerable to discovery.

The best way to explain the code is to encode something:

Take your message; e.g., the word 'TEST'. Split it into pairs of letters from the left. Then for each pair of letters take the two prime numbers corresponding to them and multiply; e.g., for 'TEST', 'TE' gives $71 \times 11 = 781$ and 'ST' gives $67 \times 71 = 4757$. So '781, 4757' is the coded message. The coded version of any message will consist of a list of numbers, half as many as there are letters in the message – assuming there is an even number of letters in the message. If there is an odd number of letters in the message, one will be left on its own at the end, and the final number in the message will just be the number corresponding to this letter. (This is probably the *Achilles' heel* of the method, as it gives away too much information and could aid someone who intercepts the message and wants to crack the code. Learners might wish to think up a better solution.) The decoder has to decide where to insert spaces to make sense of the message, which some people find the hardest element!

It will become apparent that decoding is a great deal harder than encoding and that having a calculator, though pretty essential, still doesn't make it that easy (estimation skills come into play). In mathematics (as in life generally, perhaps) it is often much harder to *undo* things than it was to *do* them! Inverse operations are often a lot more work; e.g., square rooting is a much harder process without a calculator than squaring is. In cryptography, such processes are called *trapdoor functions* (or, exaggerating a bit, *one-way functions*), because it's easy to fall through (encode) but much harder to climb back out (decode).

Related Topic
- prime factorization

Material Needed
- photocopied code sheets

Web
Go to www.50maths.com for the code sheets and a spreadsheet and program that help with encoding.

A	2
B	3
C	5
D	7
E	11
F	13
G	17
H	19
I	23
J	29
K	31
L	37
M	41
N	43
O	47
P	53
Q	59
R	61
S	67
T	71
U	73
V	79
W	83
X	89
Y	97
Z	101

1349	TH	737	SE
407	EL	869	VE
134	AS	1763	NM
2911	TM	851	IL
142	AT	851	LI
209	HE	2021	ON
82	MA	253	EI
1633	TI	323	GH
115	CI	1349	TH
86	AN	3139	UN
3337	TO	427	DR
1349	TH	77	ED
989	IN	86	AN
2201	KT	469	DS
38	HA	2047	IX
3337	TO	781	TE
473	NE	473	EN
166	WA	1349	TH
3551	SP	3431	OU
1403	RI	134	SA
451	ME	301	ND
166	WA	5893	TW
2479	SL	893	OH
33	EB	3139	UN
737	ES	427	DR
1241	GU	77	ED
11	E	86	AN
		497	DT
		437	HI
		4331	RT
		679	YD
		391	IG
		1633	IT
		67	S

There are two possible messages below, but it is easy to make your own using the spreadsheet and a program called *Primecode* provided at www.50maths.com.

Message:
THE LAST MATHEMATICIAN TO THINK THAT ONE WAS PRIME WAS LEBESGUE (1875–1941).

(Mathematicians, like many school pupils, used to think of 1 as a prime number until they 'decided' that it was better if it wasn't – in order to have 'unique factorization', as mentioned above.)

Message:
SEVENMILLIONEIGHTHUNDREDANDSIXTEENTHOUSANDTWOHUNDRED-ANDTHIRTYDIGITS

This is the number of digits in the largest known prime number (at the time of writing).

Both of these messages have been chosen to avoid an obvious ending. You don't want the ending to be guessable once you are three quarters of the way through!

Further Ideas
Learners might like to find out about the work of Bletchley Park during World War II and GCHQ and the NSA today. They could also look into public-key cryptography, trapdoor functions and the RSA algorithm.

A Single Fold

2

Paper folding can be an excellent setting in which to encourage learners to make and prove conjectures. One fold is all that is needed to provoke many possible questions, which can sometimes be quite difficult to resolve. Often this will lead to difficult manipulation of surds, but that is avoided in the scenarios below.

Take some 0.5 cm × 0.5 cm squared paper and cut out along the lines a 12 cm × 12 cm square. Make a 'corner-to-mid-point' fold, as shown below, unfold the paper and measure the various lengths created. Make some conjectures.

Related Topics
- expanding a pair of brackets
- linear equations
- Pythagoras' Theorem
- ratio
- similar triangles
- surds

Materials Needed
- plain A4 paper
- rulers
- square plain paper (21 × 21 cm) and perhaps some square squared paper (with 0.5 cm × 0.5 cm squares) the same size

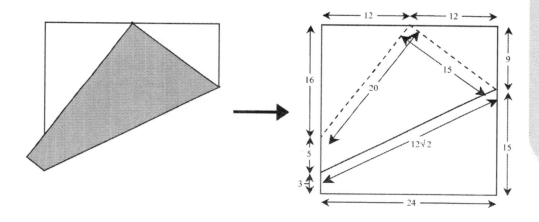

Lengths are given in units of 0.5 mm (the side length of a square).

Conjectures could simply be that the integer lengths found are exact. One way to begin a proof is to use the letter x for the length we suppose to be 9 in the diagram above, so that the length we suppose to be 15 becomes '$24 - x$'. Then, using Pythagoras' Theorem in the top right right-angled triangle leads to $x^2 + 12^2 = (24 - x)^2$. (Both top right-angled triangles are enlargements of a 3–4–5 triangle.) Learners will need to be able to expand the bracket, but, since the x^2 terms always cancel in this task, they will not need to solve any *quadratic* equations, only linear ones, such as $144 = 576 - 48x$ here. Since all the lengths are in fact exact (as can be shown by continuing in a similar way), this fold splits the left side of the square in the ratio 1:2 (8:16), and is known in origami circles as *Haga's Theorem*. It is a common way of dividing a length into thirds.

Now that we have created a position a third of the way along a side, it is tempting to iterate; i.e., to start again by folding a corner to this *new* point (the two possible corners lead to different results this time), and see where the paper meets the sides of the squares in this situation:

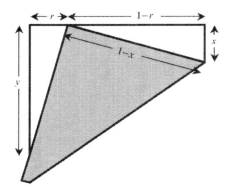

Using Pythagoras' Theorem in the top right right-angled triangle above gives $(1-r)^2 + x^2 = (1-x)^2$, and expanding, simplifying and rearranging leads to $x = r - \frac{1}{2}r^2$. (It is as well to consider values of r such as 0, ½ and 1 at this point as a check.) Using the fact that the two right-angled triangles in the diagram are similar, we can say that

$$\frac{y}{1-r} = \frac{r}{x}, \quad \text{giving} \quad y = \frac{2(1-r)}{2-r} \quad \text{and} \quad 1-y = \frac{r}{2-r},$$

so the left vertical side is split in the ratio $2(1-r):r$, or 2:1 when $r = ½$. So when $r = ⅓$, the ratio is 4:1 and when $r = ⅔$ it is 1:1. These two answers correspond to folding the two possible alternative corners up to the original ⅓ mark.

If you keep rotating the paper 90° clockwise and folding the bottom right corner up to the newly created mark, the top left fraction will go from ½ to ⅓ to ⅕ to ⅑ to 1/17; i.e., after n folds the point will be

$$\frac{1}{2^n + 1}$$

of the way along the side.

Extension

An interesting way to develop this is to use ISO-sized paper (e.g., A4) instead of square paper. Making a fold as shown on the right leads to a length such as *CD* which is *very close indeed* to 13 cm but is *not* 13 cm exactly. Calculation in a similar way to before gives

$$\frac{7\sqrt{2}}{16} \quad \text{units,}$$

taking the shorter side of the paper as 1 unit, or, scaling up by a factor of 21 cm, 12.993 . . . cm (too close to tell by measurement). (For this work you need to use the fact that the ratio of the sides of international size (like A4) paper is √2:1.) However, lengths such as *FG are exactly* 7.5 cm (5/14 units). Lots of conjectures can be made and investigated. Lines *BD* and *FH* look as though they might be parallel, which indeed they are, as can be proved by using alternate angles. The ratio *AI:IG* comes to 2:5 this time (*AI* is $^2/_7$ of the side length), and the ratio *GH:AH* comes to 5:11. The fact that the distances are too fine to call gives a motivation for proving, and yet a good thing about working with lengths on paper is that learners can keep multiplying their answers by 21 cm and measuring to check that all is going well. You can check that you're *about* right by measuring, but need algebra to be sure that you're *exactly* right.

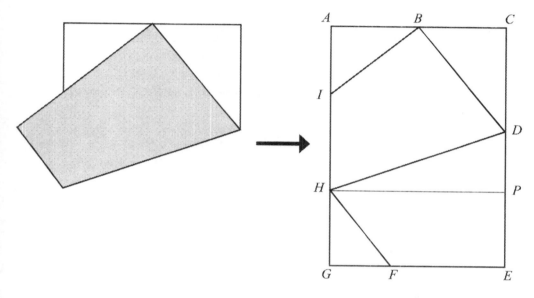

Since A4 paper is not square, there are two different 'corner-to-mid-point' folds, the other one producing 1:3 ratios on both sides.

A Single Fold Again

Related Topics

- area and perimeter
- expanding a pair of brackets
- linear equations
- Pythagoras' Theorem
- ratio
- similar triangles
- surds

Materials Needed

- plain A4 paper
- rulers

A fold that is interesting with A4 paper but not (obviously) with square paper is the 'corner-to-corner' one (* to * in the diagram below), which splits the longer sides in the ratio 1:3. The right-angled triangles produced have sides in the ratio $1: 2\sqrt{2}:3$, and similar or congruent triangles to these crop up frequently when folding ISO-sized paper.

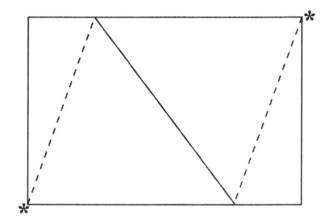

There are many opportunities here for learners to make and prove conjectures.

Another interesting move is to fold along the *diagonal* of a sheet of A4 paper, producing the following:

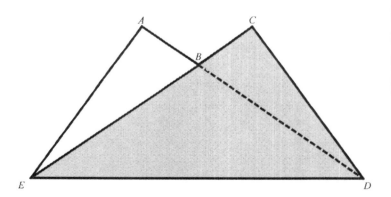

Triangles *ABE* and *BCD* are again $1: 2\sqrt{2}:3$ triangles, and the area of triangle *BDE* can be shown to be exactly *three* times the area of triangles *ABE* and *BCD*. All of this can occupy learners fruitfully for some time.

An interesting challenge is to fold a piece of A4 paper so that the remaining perimeter is rational (or an integer, even). One possible solution is to fold off isosceles right-angled triangles from opposite corners as below, although this involves making *two* folds:

The hypotenuses of the right-angled triangles are 1, so the total perimeter of the hexagon comes to

$$2(1+\frac{\sqrt{2}}{2}+(1-\frac{\sqrt{2}}{2})) = 4 \text{ units.}$$

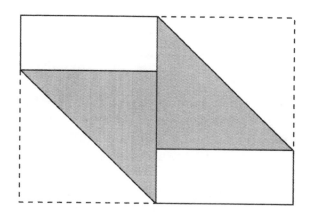

With the designs below, it is possible to make the following process a habit:

- Do the folds.
- Name the resulting shape.
- Prove that it is the shape that it looks like.
- Find its area and perimeter.
- Look for any interesting properties or questions you can ask/answer.

1 Fold off the largest possible square from a piece of A4 paper, as shown below.

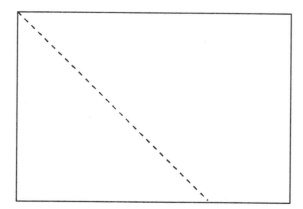

You get a right-angled trapezium with perimeter $3\sqrt{2}$ and area $\sqrt{2}-\frac{1}{2}$.

2 Fold off squares from adjacent corners of an A4 piece of paper, as shown below:

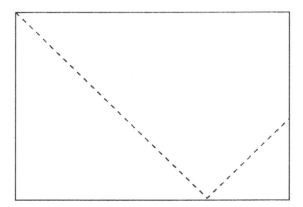

You get a kite. (It looks more like it, funnily enough, if you turn the paper over so that you can't see the folded portions.) The hypotenuse of the smaller right-angled triangle has length $\sqrt{2}(\sqrt{2}-1)$, which is equal to the remaining portion of the shorter side $(1-(\sqrt{2}-1))$. The perimeter is 4 and the area is $2(\sqrt{2}-1)$.

3 Fold a piece of A4 paper in half so that the longer sides are divided into two. Open it out again. Fold one corner in to the middle fold line, as shown below:

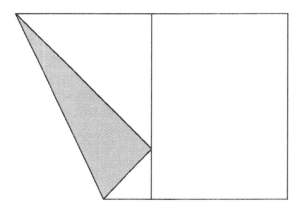

This makes a right-angled trapezium with some interesting properties, and by folding on the other side, depending on which corner you use, you can make an isosceles trapezium or a parallelogram (which looks a bit like a rhombus but isn't). Learners can, of course, be encouraged to design and then investigate their own shapes.

Silver Rectangles

What do you do with the long thin rectangles (sometimes called *silver* rectangles, although that name is also often applied to ISO-sized rectangles like A4 paper) which are the by-product of removing a 21 × 21 cm square from a sheet of A4 paper? If you do a lot of origami work, you may have quite a lot of waste 'silver change'.

1 It is a good surds exercise to confirm that the ratio of the sides of a silver rectangle is the *silver ratio* 1: $(1 + \sqrt{2})$.

2 A corner-to-corner fold produces two congruent right-angled isosceles triangles with an acute-angled isosceles triangle in between, and proving this again requires manipulation of surds.

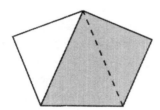

3 Try cutting the largest square possible off a silver rectangle (this is the process by which it was made from an A4 rectangle). Prove that the rectangle remaining is ISO-like (sides in the ratio 1:$\sqrt{2}$). In which step is the area scale factor of reduction greater? The answer is that the second step reduces the area by twice as much as the first step does ($2 - \sqrt{2}$ versus ½ $(2 - \sqrt{2})$).

4

Benford's Law

Related Topics

- handling data
- place value
- testing statistical hypotheses

Materials Needed

- computer spreadsheet software and internet access
- statistical packages (possibly)

Web

Go to www.50maths.com for a spreadsheet using population data.

Further Ideas

Find out about Frank Benford (1883–1948) and his law. Why does it work? How has it been used; e.g., for detecting financial crime?

Benford's Law is sufficiently counterintuitive (and unfamiliar) to create in learners at least a moderate amount of motivation to check it out for themselves. Manipulating data in the classroom can often seem pointless, since it can be tedious and has usually all been done before by other people much more carefully and using larger data samples. An exception is when the data concerns the learners themselves, but then there are often problems with the sample size not being large enough or the results being very close to what everyone would have supposed beforehand.

> *Benford's Law*: Take a list of numbers that have arisen naturally somehow (e.g., heights of mountains or amounts of money) and look at the first digit of each number. Count up how many times each digit (1 to 9) appears there and you will find that there are far more 1s than any other digit.

When Benford did it, he found that about 30% of the digits were 1s. What's special about 1? In fact the occurrence of the digits tails off as you go 1 to 9:

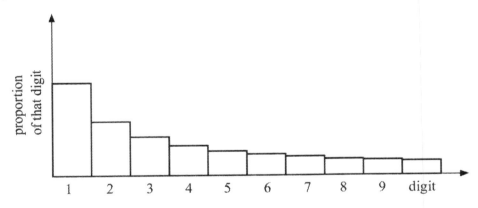

There is typically a 'No Way!' reaction from learners, or else a feeling that the numbers must have all been about the same – say, 'one thousand and something'; hence all the 1s – but that is not the case.

Data is readily available on the web for learners to test this out. Possible data sets that different learners might work with (some of which will conform very well to *Benford's Law* and some of which won't) are:

- telephone numbers (won't work)
- river lengths (OK, but should we exclude rivers over 1000 km?)

- fortunes of the world's richest people
- tables of school examination results
- population numbers
- numbers of pupils in school form groups (won't work because the numbers will be too similar)
- heights of the world's tallest buildings (won't work very well, since all are over a certain height and not that varied – the same problem arises with human heights or IQ scores)
- random numbers (won't work at all)

Learners can hunt around for lists of numbers, perhaps relating to their interests, and try them out. The units for measurements won't matter so long as they are all the same. Spreadsheet formulae such as *=LEFT(A3)* are useful for acquiring the left-hand digit (the *leading digit*) of the number in cell A3, and *=COUNTIF(B$1:B$1000,C3)* is a convenient way of counting the number of occurrences of a digit (equal to the number in C3) in a list (going from B1 to B1000).

5

Can We Play A Game?

Related Topics
- square numbers
- strategy

Materials Needed
- counters (e.g., cubes, paperclips or spent matchsticks)

Web
For an interactive version of the coin problem, go to http://nlvm.usu.edu/en/nav/frames_asid_139_g_3_t_2.html, which does 8, 9 and 12 coins.

Further Idea
Find out about the game *Nim* and its variations.

The 180 Game

Start with 180.
Each player in turn has to subtract any square number less than the current total.
The player who makes zero wins.
So a possible game could go

Player 1: $180 - 64 = 116$
Player 2: $116 - 36 = 80$
Player 1: $80 - 9 = 71$
Player 2: $71 - 64 = 7$
Player 1: $7 - 1 = 6$
Player 2: $6 - 4 = 2$
Player 1: $2 - 1 = 1$
Player 2: $1 - 1 = 0$ and wins.

- What's the best way to play this game?
- Could Player 1 have won by starting differently? Or playing different moves later? *Yes. In fact, if you always aim for one of the 'magic' numbers in the following list, you are guaranteed to win. You can always get to at least one of them from any number in the game, provided that it is not on the list! Since 180 is in the list, it means that Player 2 should win if both players play as well as possible.*

2, 5, 7, 10, 12, 15, 17, 20, 22, 34, 39, 44, 52, 57, 62, 65, 67, 72, 85, 95, 109, 119, 124, 127, 130, 132, 137, 142, 147, 150, 170, 177, 180. (This list consists of all the numbers in this range which *can't* be made by adding square numbers to numbers already in the list.)

- What if it is the person who makes zero who *loses*? *You just need to add one to the numbers in the list and aim for those numbers instead.*

The Dodgy Coin

This is a well-known type of problem and there are some interactive versions on the internet; e.g., http://nlvm.usu.edu/en/nav/frames_asid_139_g_3_t_2.html, which does 8, 9 and 12 coins.

You have eight coins of the same mass and one that is lighter, but they all look the same. You have to find which is the lighter one by using a simple scales balance.

- What is the smallest number of weighings that will always be enough?
- What if there are a different number of coins?
- What if you don't know whether the dodgy coin is heavier or lighter than the rest?

number of coins	minimum number of weighings	procedure
8	2	Weigh 3 against 3; if they balance, one of the two remaining coins must be the light one, so weigh them against each other to see which one it is. If they *don't* balance, take the lighter group of 3 and choose any 2 of them. Weigh them against each other; if one is lighter, then that is the one; if they balance, then the unweighed one must be the one.
9	2	The same sort of procedure for 8 will work for 9.
12	3	Weigh 4 against 4; if they balance, take the unweighed 4; if one side is lighter, take this group of 4. So in the first weighing you have definitely established the group of 4 in which the dodgy coin lies. It now seems to take two more weighings (2 against 2 and 1 against 1) to find the dodgy coin. However, it is possible to do the whole thing in 3 weighings, even if you don't know whether the dodgy coin is heavier or lighter (see Long, C. T. (1992) Magic in Base 3, *Mathematical Gazette*, Vol 76, 477, November, or, for an easier practical way, www.cut-the-knot. org/blue/OddCoinProblems.shtml)!

6

Catch 22

Related Topics
- place value
- proof

Many surprising numerical results require fairly complicated algebra to prove, quite often multiplication of brackets. One that doesn't, and can be accessible from Year 7 upwards, is the following:

Choose any three integers between 1 and 9.

Make all the possible 2-digit numbers that you can using these digits (only once each).

For example, with 2, 5 and 8 you can make 25, 52, 28, 82, 58, 85.

Add these up and you get 330.

Add up the three original numbers and you get $2 + 5 + 8 = 15$.

Divide 330 by 15 and you get *22*.

Do the same thing with a different set of three starting numbers.

You get 22 again.

Why 22? Will this always happen?

It can be useful to encourage learners to make it a habit to consider what might be altered about a problem to make it easier (to get started), or harder (to be suitably challenging) or just different (for interest). The two obvious variables here are the number of numbers chosen at the start and the length (e.g., 2-digit) of the numbers being formed. For example, starting with *four* numbers (but still making all the possible 2-digit numbers out of them), the final answer comes to 33, inviting the prediction that with n starting numbers the final value will be $11(n-1)$, which turns out to be correct.

- What if you make 3-digit or 4-digit numbers, etc?

A full generalization is that with n starting numbers, and making all the possible r-digit numbers, the final value comes to

$$\frac{(n-1)!(10^r - 1)}{9(n-r)!}.$$

This may also be written as

$$\frac{(n-1)!R_r}{(n-r)!},$$

where R_r is the rth 'repunit' ($R_1 = 1$, $R_2 = 11$, $R_3 = 111$, $R_r = \dfrac{10^r - 1}{9}$, etc).

Answers for some values of n and r are shown in the table below:

number of starting numbers (n)

number of digits in numbers created (r)	1	2	3	4	5	6	7	8	9	10
1	1	1	1	1	1	1	1	1	1	1
2		11	22	33	44	55	66	77	88	99
3			222	666	1332	2220	3330	4662	6216	7992
4				6666	26664	66660	133320	233310	373296	559944
5					266664	1333320	3999960	9333240	18666480	33599664
6						13333320	79999920	279999720	746665920	1679998320
7							799999920	5599999440	22399997760	67199993280

The symbolism of 666, along with the 'Catch 22' nature of the initial problem, may be striking if learners try 3-digit numbers from four numbers as their second example!

There are a lot of possible patterns to explore here. Proving can be done, if desired, without much recourse to algebra. If algebra *is* used, there are opportunities for exhaustive systematic thinking and plenty of collecting terms.

Let the (three) starting numbers be a, b and c and write the possible 2-digit numbers as

$10a + b$
$10b + a$
$10a + c$
$10c + a$
$10b + c$
$10c + b$

There will be ^nP_r possibilities and $\dfrac{^nP_r}{n}$ occurrences of each of the terms $10a$, $10b$, $10c$, a, b and c, making, in total,

$$\frac{^nP_r}{n}(a+b+c)(1+10+10^2 + \ldots +10^{r-1}),$$

leading to the given result

$$\frac{(n-1)!(10^r -1)}{9(n-r)!}.$$

Extension

Learners might try to create and analyse a different but similar problem, perhaps involving subtraction or multiplication.

7

Colourful Expressions

Related Topics
- algebraic expressions
- formulae
- sequences

Materials Needed
- coloured cubes may be helpful
- coloured pencils or pens

Web
A colour version of the table is available at www.50maths.com.

Caution
Is anyone colour blind?

Algebraic *'expressions'* are often handled by pupils in an attempt to get 'the right answer', defined as one that will satisfy a teacher, rather than as a tool to *'express'* something meaningful. An answer to the question 'Is this the right expression?' might be 'Well, does it express what you are trying to say?' Algebra is a powerful, concise, elegant but difficult language, yet it exists to express meaningful relationships, and that is what the topic of algebraic expressions should be all about.

One way to make a closer link between the symbols and what they symbolize is to use tables of coloured numbers to represent different variables:

black	red	yellow	green	blue	purple
1	4	2	10	3	16
2	5	4	9	5	25
3	6	6	8	7	36
4	7	8	7	9	49
5	8	10	6	11	64

(A colour version of this is available at www.50maths.com.)

The colours encourage statements to be made linking 'the red numbers' with 'the yellow numbers', say – perhaps first in words and then in 'word equations', as 'function machines' and in symbols; e.g.,

words: 'You take the red number and minus three and then double it to get the yellow number.'

'word equation': yellow $= 2 \times ($red $- 3)$

'function machines': red $\rightarrow \boxed{-3} \rightarrow \boxed{\times 2} \rightarrow$ yellow

algebra: $y = 2(r - 3)$

It might not be possible to go all the way to algebra straight away, but expressing general relationships in words can be a step towards fuller abstraction.

With five colours, there are $^5C_2 = 10$ possible pairs of colours to link (and 20 if you count in both directions), some of which will be challenging, and by using more than two of the colours at once complex connections can be found. A possible homework task (well differentiated by outcome) is to ask learners to construct their own tables, containing numbers of their own choice, together with a given number of accompanying 'connections statements' in one form or another.

Some learners will be more comfortable with inductive statements such as 'The yellow numbers go up in twos'. Questions such as 'What have the yellow numbers got to do with the black numbers?' or 'How do you turn a black number yellow?', say, choosing a helpful colour, such as black here, may encourage a deductive approach.

Often learners wish to keep the colours for a while, always writing 'r', say, in red, or at least thinking of it as red. You may be asked what colour 'x' is supposed to be! (The name 'Xanthe' means yellow, so is a possible answer to this!) I am happy to trust learners to discard this model when they are ready.

A related model is to link a letter with a learner's name, so that k is taken to be Kyle's number, say. This can be helpful for either a specific unknown (Kyle is thinking of a number or numbers) or a variable (Kyle's values). Where a coloured letter stands for an unknown, red can be 'how many red cubes I've got in my pocket' or 'what number is in the red envelope'.

Coordinate Transformations

Start with any simple unsymmetrical shape drawn between lattice points on a coordinate grid; e.g.

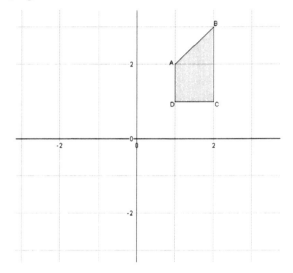

Say that you're going to add 3 to both coordinates of every vertex of the shape. What will happen to the shape?

It is often a surprise to learners that the shape doesn't get any bigger, just translates $\binom{3}{3}$.

• What would need to be done to the coordinates to achieve other translations? How could you make the shape bigger?

This generalizes, for positive or negative a and b, so that $(x, y) \rightarrow (x+a, y+b)$ corresponds to a translation $\binom{a}{b}$.

You could get to this point as a whole class and then set off into group/individual work on the following:

• Make up some rules about how you are going to change the coordinates and then do some drawings to find out what happens. Try to summarize your results in words or pictures or algebra. Try simple things first!

(The opposite approach is also possible: do some transformations and see what happens to the coordinates. However, small inaccuracies can lead to false values for the coordinates and it can become a headache trying to sort out what is genuine and what spurious. If you want to take this direction it may be better to use dynamic geometry software in order to get precise results.)

Common ideas might include:

- swap around the x and y coordinates
- double both coordinates
- multiply the x-coordinate by 3 and leave the y-coordinate alone
- make the y-coordinate minus what it was and leave the x-coordinate alone
- take each coordinate away from 10

For some transformations learners will need to extend the axes further. It may be best for everyone to stick with the class shape that you began with, but if learners do use other shapes it is best if they are unsymmetrical ones, otherwise some transformations will not 'show up'. Learners could make posters or presentations illustrating what 'their' transformation does.

Here are some possible results:

transformation	$(x, y) \longrightarrow$
reflection in x-axis	$(x, -y)$
reflection in y-axis	$(-x, y)$
rotation 180° about (0, 0)	$(-x, -y)$
reflection in $y = x$	(y, x)
rotation 90° clockwise about (0, 0)	$(y, -x)$
rotation 90° anticlockwise about (0, 0)	$(-y, x)$
rotation 90° clockwise about (a, b)	$(a - b + y, a + b - x)$
rotation 90° anticlockwise about (a, b)	$(a + b - y, b - a + x)$
reflection in $y = -x$	$(-y, -x)$
enlargement, scale factor k, centre (0, 0)	(kx, ky)
enlargement, scale factor k, centre (a, b)	$(kx - (k-1)a, ky - (k-1)b)$

There is no limit to how far this investigation might go, since learners may think of non-linear transformations such as

$$(x, y) \longrightarrow (\frac{1}{x}, y^2),$$

with all kinds of interesting results! For transformations of the form $(x, y) \longrightarrow (mx + a, ny + b)$, the geometrical result may be seen more easily in stages:

$$(x, y) \longrightarrow (mx, y) \longrightarrow (mx, ny) \longrightarrow (mx + a, ny) \longrightarrow (mx + a, ny + b)$$

stretch in x-dir   stretch in y-dir   translation $\binom{a}{0}$ translation $\binom{0}{b}$
scale factor m scale factor n

Seating plan

You will need to adapt this according to the seating arrangements in your classroom. It can, incidentally, be a convenient way of mixing pupils up without their attention being on why they are being asked to sit somewhere else! For *reflection*, you can use a stick (such as a window-opening pole) or just your arm to indicate a straight line through the room. 'Ryan, I want you to reflect in that line.' Whoever is sitting where Ryan moves to also has to reflect back into Ryan's seat. (The rule is that when someone 'lands' on your seat, you have to move by doing the same transformation they have done.)

Rotation is more interesting. Depending on your seating structure, you may be able to do it 'round' a whole classroom, but if pupils are sitting around separate islands of tables, it works best. All sorts of questions may arise, such as: 'How many people will have to shift if I ask Jaskiran to rotate 90° anticlockwise around this point?' If some seats are empty, that can add interesting complications.

Translations lead to a 'domino effect', so only work where there is eventually an empty seat (unless someone jumps out of the window!). 'Who in this room could do a translation without our losing anybody out of the window?!'

Digital Roots

To find the *digital root* of an integer, work out the sum of its digits (its *digit sum*) and if the answer has more than one digit work out *its* digit sum. Keep going until you have a one-digit answer. That is the digital root of the original number (and, incidentally, of all the numbers encountered along the way).

Learners could begin investigating digital roots by making a digital root tables square from 1 to 9:

1	2	3	4	5	6	7	8	9
2	4	6	8	1	3	5	7	9
3	6	9	3	6	9	3	6	9
4	8	3	7	2	6	1	5	9
5	1	6	2	7	3	8	4	9
6	3	9	6	3	9	6	3	9
7	5	3	1	8	6	4	2	9
8	7	6	5	4	3	2	1	9
9	9	9	9	9	9	9	9	9

Related Topics
- divisibility tests
- properties of numbers

Web
For a spreadsheet digital roots table square and a page of '9-point circles', go to www.50maths.com.

Further Idea
Find out what 'casting out nines' is/was. What does it mean to say that you will get 'false positives' with this method about one time in nine that you use it?

What conjectures can you make, test and prove concerning the digital roots of:

- **multiples of different numbers?** *All multiples of 9 (except zero) have digital roots of 9; all multiples of 3 (except zero) have digital roots of 3, 6 or 9. Learners could work on finding rules for which multiples of 3 have which digital root. (If the multiple of 3 is 3 less than a multiple of 9, its digital root is 6; if it is 3 more than a multiple of 9, its digital root is 3.)*
- **square numbers?** *Always 1, 4, 7 or 9.* Is there a pattern to when these occur?
- **cube numbers?** *Always 1, 8 or 9.* Is there a pattern to when these occur?
- **triangle numbers?** *Always 1, 3, 6 or 9.* Is there a pattern to when these occur?
- **prime numbers?** *Anything except 6 or 9 or (except for 3 itself) 3.*

Learners might investigate whatever other kinds of numbers they are familiar with; e.g., perfect numbers (always 1, except for 6); powers of 2 (anything except 3, 6 or 9); factorials (1, 2, 6, 6, 3 and then 9 for all the rest, since 9 is a factor of all factorials from 6! onwards).

- What kinds of numbers have a digital root of 4, say? *Numbers which are 4 more than a multiple of 9. If the digital root of a number is not 9, then it is equal to the remainder after dividing the number by 9.*
- How many *steps* does it take to get to the digital root? (This is called the *additive persistence* of the number.)

Extensions

1 Using a circle which has its circumference divided evenly into nine portions (a page of these is available at www.50maths.com), number the points clockwise 1 to 9. Choose a row (or column) in the table above and join the point corresponding to the first number to that corresponding to the second number. Continue to the third number, and so on, until you arrive back at the point you started at. Different lines in the table produce various interesting and attractive patterns.

2 A different visual representation of digital roots is to use squared paper and begin in the centre with a line equal in length (number of squares) to the first number in the row (or column) of the table above. Then turn the paper 90° clockwise and continue with a line equal in length to the next number in the table. Keep going, rotating 90° clockwise (learners need to keep turning the paper in the *same* sense – this can be difficult) each time, until you get back to the starting point. The finished drawing is a *spirolateral* (see below). (These are easy to create using *Logo*.) The patterns produced can provoke interesting comments relating to symmetry.

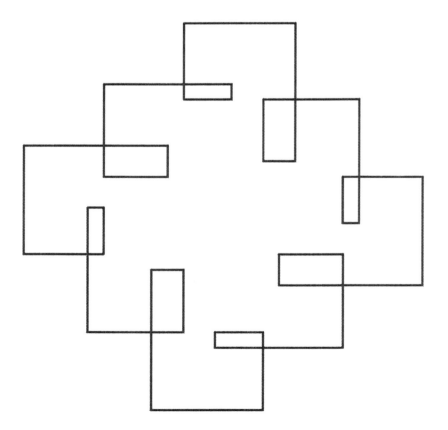

Dot To Dot

10

There are 49 (7^2) integer coordinate points (lattice points) on the grid to the right.

Choose five points (five different learners might choose them) and join every point to every other point. (You need to be careful that you really have done this and not missed out any connections!)

For example, (1, 5), (2, 3), (3, 1), (3, 3), (5, 3). (See the diagram below right.)

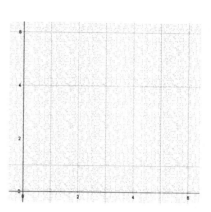

- **How many straight lines are there?** *Here we would count only 6 lines. It doesn't matter if a line goes through a coordinate point. We are counting the minimum number of times you would have to place your ruler on the page to draw the figure: only 6 times here.*
- **With a different choice of coordinates, could we have got a different number of lines? What different numbers of lines are possible with five points? (The five points must all be different distinct points; you cannot count the same point more than once.)** *With 5 points you can get 1, 5, 6, 8 or 10 lines.*

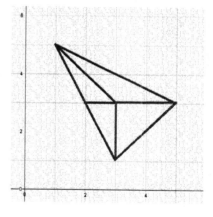

Learners may find it easier to envisage moving the points in the diagram to the right, creating or destroying lines. A more tactile way of doing this might be with drawing pins and elastic bands.

The task is intended to encourage thinking about gradient, since when three points are collinear (all on a straight line) the gradient of the line joining any two is the same.

The maximum possible number of lines will be $^5C_2 = 10$; e.g., if the points lie at the vertices of a regular pentagon. The minimum possible number will obviously be 1 if they all lie on a single straight line.

number of points	possible numbers of lines
1	1
2	1
3	1, 3
4	1, 4, 6
5	1, 5, 6, 8, 10
6	1, 6, 7, 8, 9, 10, 11, 13, 15

Related Topics
- coordinates
- gradient
- triangle numbers

- Can you predict without drawing (shut your eyes if it helps) how many lines there are going to be in certain cases? Start with 'easy' coordinates, such as (0, 0), (1, 1), (2, 2), (3, 3), (4, 4) – one line.

As learners become comfortable generalizing, larger numbers in the coordinates will present fewer problems, provided they are carefully chosen; e.g., (0, 0), (10, 10), (57, 57), (100, 100), (20, 40) is five lines. (a, b), (c, d) and (e, f) lie on a straight (non-vertical) line if

$$\frac{d-b}{c-a} = \frac{f-d}{e-c}$$

(assuming that c is not equal to a or e).

Extension

- A different problem involves choosing your five points and then wiping them out with the smallest number of 'straight-line wipes'. (This works well on a whiteboard and is a bit like playing a game like *Connect-4*[8]. You draw the dots and then, moving your finger along the board in a straight line, rub out as many as you can.) The aim is to remove all the dots with as few 'shots' as necessary. *You will never need more than three wipes, because you can do at least two dots in each go, and 5/2 rounded up is 3. In general, an upper bound for n dots is*

$$\left\lceil \frac{n}{2} \right\rceil,$$

where the $\lceil \ \rceil$ brackets mean 'round up to the nearest integer'.

- This problem might remind learners of the classic puzzle where you are asked to draw four straight lines without taking your pen off the paper so that you go through all the dots in a 3×3 array. (With a 4×4 array it is possible to do it in 6 lines; with a 5×5 it takes 8 lines and with a 6×6 it takes 10.)

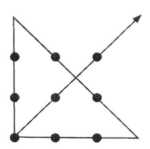

Every Number From One Letter

11

As a class, choose a small positive integer, such as 3, and a letter of the alphabet, such as f, and declare that $f = 3$.

The task now is to write an algebraic expression to make every number from 1 to 100 (different groups/individuals can be assigned different ranges of numbers). The catch is that the answer must not be 'obvious'. How this will be interpreted will vary, but making 4 by writing '$f + 1$', 5 by writing '$f + 2$', etc, is clearly not ambitious enough! Possible guidelines you might negotiate with the class could be:

- it must be something for which it would be sensible to use a calculator; or
- *without* a calculator, it must take the teacher more than 10 seconds but less than 30 seconds to work it out; or
- it must contain at least three different mathematical symbols; or
- it must be too hard to be done by an average member of Year $(n - 1)$ (where n is the year group of the class), etc.

The aim is to impress by your inventiveness rather than to complete the numbers assigned to you as quickly as possible. Aim to surprise, to show off what you know about, to think of something few others will think of, to produce something particularly 'elegant', etc. (You could take examples from learners, but it sometimes happens that if you do and you particularly praise one idea then you end up getting a lot of that, which can be limiting.)

One approach is to start by doing things to f and seeing what numbers you end up with, filling in the gaps later on, rather than picking a random number, such as 73, and spending a lot of time failing to make it. Learners may be encouraged if you point out that when you fail you at least make another number that may be in your range. The fact that you are working towards a *range* can encourage good estimation work.

In a plenary, groups or individuals can share 'your most impressive idea' or 'the expression you're proudest of' or 'the one you spent longest thinking about' or 'your most unusual one', etc. Some answers display a sense of symmetry and beauty; e.g.,

- $f + f^2 + f^3 = 39$
- $f^4 + 4f + 4 = 97$

Identities such as $4f \equiv f + f + f + f$ and equations such as

$$\frac{f^4}{9} = f^2$$

are often by-products of this task, and collecting these together can be a good task for those who finish early.

Expressions of value

- Define the values of four letters on the board; e.g., $a = 4$, $b = -2$, $c = 0$, $d = \frac{1}{10}$. Then ask learners to say aloud (or write on a mini-whiteboard) connections between them; e.g.,

$$\frac{a + b}{20} = d.$$

Everybody has to think of one. This can be very well differentiated by outcome, with learners choosing to articulate relationships with which they are comfortable.
- The task in this lesson can be thought of as an algebraic parallel to 'Four Fours', where learners are asked to make all the integers from 1 to 20 using just a maximum of four 4s (and any other mathematical symbols, depending on the particular rules). If they are not familiar with that, it could be a related task to use (see Foster, *Instant Maths Ideas, 1*, page 48).

Every Possible Answer

Teaching 'order of operations' (using BIDMAS or its variations) can be very dull if learners are merely required to compute an excessive number of tedious and contrived calculations for no purpose other than 'practice'. (In practice, many 'professional' mathematicians frequently insert 'unnecessary' brackets in order to clarify their meaning, so it is possible to overestimate the importance of this topic.) Embedding this work in a problem-solving puzzle context can make it a bit more interesting. There is generally more thinking needed if learners have to construct calculations to arrive at given answers rather than the other way round.

Related Topics
• fractions
• priority of operations

Web
There is a spreadsheet to help with marking/discussion at www.50maths.com.
There is a continued fraction calculator at www.mcs.surrey.ac.uk/Personal/R.Knott/Fibonacci/cfCALC.html.

- Using the symbols $+ - \times \div$ only (repeats allowed) and the numbers 1, 2 and 3 (once each; repeats *not* allowed), how many possible calculations can you write down?
- How many different possible answers do they make?

It might be worth being clear at the outset whether *concatenation* (putting digits alongside each other; e.g., making 32 from 2 and 3) is or isn't allowed. Brackets are expressly not allowed, since otherwise they tend to be overused.

Assuming no concatenation, there are just $3! = 6$ arrangements of the three numbers, and for each of those arrangements any of the four operation symbols can be placed in either of the two gaps in $4^2 = 16$ possible ways, making 96 possible calculations altogether. That is a lot, but not if the work is divided among different groups within the class. (This can lead to a double benefit of learners having a purpose in explaining their results to one another rather than doing it merely to oblige the teacher.) When you work these out, there are only 24 different answers, ranging from −5 to 7, the most common answer being 6 (16 times).

- How can you get the biggest/smallest possible answer?
- What can we change about this task?
- What if we start with a different three numbers?
- What if two of the numbers are the same? Or all three? *It is easier to begin with repeated numbers; e.g., with 999, there are only 11 different possible answers.*
- Can you choose the starting numbers so that you obtain certain answers; e.g., the prime numbers?

Some hard challenges are possible.

Extension

An interesting task for practising calculator use in this context is to evaluate *continued fractions*; the pay-off being some surprising answers (try guessing before you start roughly the size of the answer – it is very difficult).

- For example, try this sequence:

$$\cfrac{1}{1+\cfrac{1}{2}} = \frac{2}{3}, \quad \cfrac{1}{1+\cfrac{1}{1+\cfrac{1}{2}}} = \frac{3}{5}, \quad \cfrac{1}{1+\cfrac{1}{1+\cfrac{1}{1+\cfrac{1}{2}}}} = \frac{5}{8}, \quad \cfrac{1}{1+\cfrac{1}{1+\cfrac{1}{1+\cfrac{1}{1+\cfrac{1}{2}}}}} = \frac{8}{13}, \text{ etc.}$$

You don't have to start afresh each time; all you need to do is $\cfrac{1}{1+ previous}$,

which explains why the Fibonacci numbers appear in the answers. (The answers are getting closer and closer to the reciprocal of the golden mean.)

- You can't use that trick with this one:

$$\cfrac{1}{1+\cfrac{1}{2}} = \frac{2}{3}, \quad \cfrac{1}{1+\cfrac{1}{2+\cfrac{1}{3}}} = \frac{7}{10}, \quad \cfrac{1}{1+\cfrac{1}{2+\cfrac{1}{3+\cfrac{1}{4}}}} = \frac{30}{43}, \quad \cfrac{1}{1+\cfrac{1}{2+\cfrac{1}{3+\cfrac{1}{4+\cfrac{1}{5}}}}} = \frac{157}{225}, \text{ etc.}$$

Working some of these out without a calculator requires/develops strong skills with fractions! But the main idea is to be using a calculator yet thinking carefully about the order in which you do things.

- Can you start with a 'normal' fraction, say ⁵/₁₂, and convert it to a continued fraction? *The answer is*

$$\cfrac{1}{1+\cfrac{1}{2+\cfrac{1}{2}}}$$

and one way to find it is to convert the starting fraction to a decimal (⁵/₁₂ = 0.416 …), subtract the integer part (0), reciprocal what is left (1 ÷ 0.416 … = 2.4), subtract the integer part (2), reciprocal what is left (1 ÷ 0.4 = 2.5), subtract the integer part (2), reciprocal what is left (1 ÷ 0.5 = 2), subtract the integer part (2), until, as here, you have nothing left. The integer parts that you subtracted, in order, are the numbers you need for your continued fraction.

Chemistry

Compare the conventions, such as brackets, in *chemical* formulae with those used in algebra; e.g., in a chemical equation such as $CaCO_3 + 2HNO_3 \rightarrow Ca(NO_3)_2 + H_2O + CO_2$, the big number 2 in front of HNO_3 means two moles of nitric acid, whereas the subscript 3 in HNO_3 means three oxygen atoms only. The subscript 2 in $Ca(NO_3)_2$ means two nitrate (NO_3^-) ions, and although that would be the same as $N_2O_6^{2-}$ in total atom count, it is expressing something different chemically.

13   Farey Sequences

Related Topics
- coordinates
- fractions
- gradient
- rational and irrational numbers
- straight-line graphs

Materials Needed
- calculators
- protractors (possibly)
- squared paper

One of the trickiest things about fractions is the fact that you can write infinitely many fractions that are equal to each other (e.g., $^2/_5$, $^4/_{10}$, $^1/_{2.5}$, $^{-2000}/_{-5000}$, etc). Learners can enjoy making up more and more outlandish fractions equal to a given fraction – every pupil has to say one that hasn't been said before, trying to be as inventive as possible. However, while it may not be hard to generate correct answers, really seeing that they are *the same number* is not easy.

Since a fraction contains two numbers, it is tempting to plot them as coordinates:

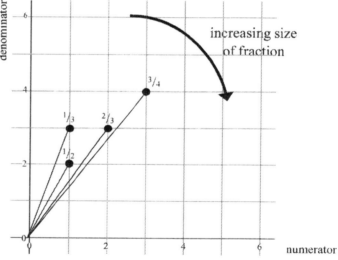

The advantage of having the numerator on the horizontal axis and the denominator on the vertical, as here, is that the numbers come in the same order as you read (and write) a fraction: top then bottom; along then up. However, it means that the 'top number' of the fraction (the numerator) is on the 'bottom', horizontal axis, and the denominator axis 'goes up', which can be awkward. Also, the gradient of each line is the reciprocal of the value of the fraction rather than the value itself, so you might wish to do it the other way round.

Ask learners to plot a few fractions and then study the diagram:

- 'Say what you see', 'Comment on any patterns'.

Equivalent fractions lie along straight lines through the origin, so a number is not really represented by a *point* but by a *line* (extending the other side of the origin to include fractions such as $^{-2}/_{-6}$). The fraction in lowest terms is represented by the grid point (in the first quadrant) closest to the origin that lies on the line. The gradient of the line is the reciprocal of the value of the fraction (or equal to it if you plot the numerator and denominator the other way round).

Possible questions might be:

- Where is your biggest/smallest fraction?
- Who's got a bigger/smaller fraction than that? Where is it?
- Invent a bigger/smaller fraction. Where would it be?
- Where is zero? *The answer is anywhere along the denominator axis except the origin.*

The nearer the line is to the numerator axis, the larger the fraction; the nearer to the denominator axis, the smaller the fraction. No matter how big the fraction, the line will never rotate past the numerator axis. The only way to make a line that will leave this quadrant is to use one negative number and one positive, so fractions less than zero correspond to lines with negative gradients.

A good task is to ask pupils to make *Farey Sequences*. The fourth Farey Sequence, for instance, is the list (in order of increasing size) of all the simplified fractions between 0 and 1 which you can make using integers less than or equal to 4; i.e., $^0\!/_1$, $^1\!/_4$, $^1\!/_3$, $^1\!/_2$, $^2\!/_3$, $^3\!/_4$, $^1\!/_1$. Learners could work out the first six Farey Sequences, say, using their diagram, perhaps checking on a calculator.

$F_1 = \{^0\!/_1, ^1\!/_1\}$
$F_2 = \{^0\!/_1, ^1\!/_2, ^1\!/_1\}$
$F_3 = \{^0\!/_1, ^1\!/_3, ^1\!/_2, ^2\!/_3, ^1\!/_1\}$
$F_4 = \{^0\!/_1, ^1\!/_4, ^1\!/_3, ^1\!/_2, ^2\!/_3, ^3\!/_4, ^1\!/_1\}$
$F_5 = \{^0\!/_1, ^1\!/_5, ^1\!/_4, ^1\!/_3, ^2\!/_5, ^1\!/_2, ^3\!/_5, ^2\!/_3, ^3\!/_4, ^4\!/_5, ^1\!/_1\}$
$F_6 = \{^0\!/_1, ^1\!/_6, ^1\!/_5, ^1\!/_4, ^1\!/_3, ^2\!/_5, ^1\!/_2, ^3\!/_5, ^2\!/_3, ^3\!/_4, ^4\!/_5, ^5\!/_6, ^1\!/_1\}$

Except for the first one, they all have an odd number of terms and the middle one is always $^1\!/_2$.

Learners can join up their fractions in order of size to make a zigzag line heading in the direction of the numerator axis; e.g., below, for the sixth Farey Sequence. Why will the line never cross itself?

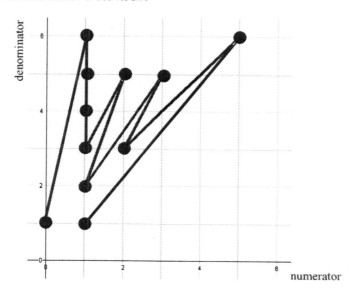

Further Ideas
The *Stern–Brocot Tree* gives a diagrammatic picture of Farey Sequences, and a set of *Ford circles* can provide a beautiful illustration. (There are numerous links to these on the web.)
Find out who John Farey (1766–1826) was; he wasn't a mathematician.

Extension

- Add/subtract two fractions and plot the answer. Where is it? *The answer to* $a/b \pm c/d$ *is anywhere except the origin on the line*

$$y = \frac{ac}{bc \pm ad} x,$$

provided (for subtraction) that $bc - ad \neq 0$, *in which case the two fractions are equal and the answer is zero (i.e. on the denominator axis).*

- What fraction is 'half way between on the grid' $\frac{1}{3}$ and $\frac{2}{3}$, say? *The answer is* $\frac{1}{2}$, *the mean of the two fractions.* Does this always work? *No.* Try other points.

The value of the fraction at the point midway between two points is the *mediant* of the two fractions; i.e., if the fractions are a/b and c/d, the mediant is

$$\frac{a+c}{b+d}.$$

Since learners have a tendency to write this as the answer to the *sum* of a/b and c/d, this can be a good context for exposing that misconception, since the mediant is *always too small* to be the sum. In fact, it always lies in size between the two fractions (assuming they are not equal), as can be seen by its position on the grid.

Fermi Questions

Fermi Questions are order of magnitude calculations which involve estimating any necessary values to get a ballpark figure. One of Fermi's original ones was 'How many piano tuners are there in New York?' Creating and solving problems like this can be fun, especially when the answers confound our expectations – and the 'No way!' factor is a good motivation for checking whatever someone else claims.

A nice way of structuring this work is for learners to make quizzes for one another, perhaps multiple choice (even 'Yes/No'). Or this work could form a competition in aid of charity – a more interesting version of the familiar 'How many coins are there in this jar?' type of question. It can take learners a while to become comfortable with doing rough calculations where (for once in maths lessons) they are not supposed to be trying to be accurate. Common sense is needed in making assumptions and adopting a 'back-of-an-envelope' mentality.

You could supply 'random' but suggestive data: 'What questions can you ask using this data?' Where a necessary piece of information is not readily available, making appropriate assumptions is all part of the process, either guesstimating or searching on the internet. It is important that learners do not use the web uncritically, as, in this sort of area in particular, there is a lot of inaccurate and misleading information confidently presented! Estimation is a vital life skill for knowing who and what to believe in today's world.

Here is some possible raw data that you could supply and see what learners can do with it:

- A newsreader speaks 3 words a second.
- The British Library possesses 150 million items.
- There are 250 million bubbles in a bottle of champagne and about 2000 in a bar of Aero® chocolate.
- A tennis court is 78 feet by 36 feet. A football pitch is 200 yards by 100 yards. (How many people could comfortably stand on either?)
- A marathon is 26 miles 385 yards.
- Altogether in the world there are 10^{23} grains of sand, 10^{30} bacteria, 10^{47} molecules of water and 10^{50} atoms.
- There are 10^{12} bacteria on the surface of the human body and 10^{15} inside. The body contains 10^{14} cells (so 10 times more bacteria than cells!) and nearly 10^{28} atoms.

Related Topics
- estimation
- rounding
- standard form
- units

Materials Needed
- computers (possibly)
- data (see below)

Further Ideas
Find out about Enrico Fermi (1901–54) and try some of his original questions. Choose an animal, research some of its 'statistics' and compare with humans.

- An average pencil can be sharpened 17 times and can write 45 000 words or draw a line 56 km long.
- Fingernails grow at a rate of 0.1 mm per day (toenails at about a third of the speed). An average head contains about 100 000 hairs, which grow at about 0.4 mm per day. (How long would you have to leave your hair growing before it reached the floor? How long would it grow in a lifetime?)
- Populations:

country	population (2007 estimates)
(World)	(6.6 billion)
China	1.3 billion
India	1.1 billion
US	301 million
UK	60.8 million
Australia	20.4 million

- Humans versus ants:

	ants	humans
average mass	20 mg	70 kg
mass of brain	0.3 mg	1.5 kg
world population	10 000 000 000 000 000 ($= 10^{16}$)	6.6 billion
number of brain cells	250 000	100 billion
lifetime	50 days (some much longer – it depends on the kind)	100 years

- There are 52 billion chickens in the world.
- It takes the whole lifetimes of 12 bees to make 1 teaspoon of honey, and bees travel a total of 75 000 km to make a pound of honey.

Fibonacci Grids

15

Offer learners the grid below (there is a copy at www.50maths.com) or one like it and ask, 'What do you notice?' or 'Describe something you see', or invite them to, 'Talk about a pattern that you spot'. Try to accept straightforward replies like 'numbers' and continue with, 'Anything else?' rather than implying that some answers are too obvious; it should not feel like 'Guess what the teacher is getting at' but a genuine interest in what features appear significant to the learner at that moment.

7	18	25	43	68
4	11	15	26	41
3	7	10	**17**	27
1	4	5	9	14
2	3	5	8	13

Anyone who quickly thinks they see exactly what is going on could be challenged to make another table of a similar kind – it will come in handy later.

If I covered up some numbers, could you work out what they were? How many numbers could I hide? How much would you have to *memorize* if I was going to rub this out and you had to reproduce it exactly?

The rule by which the table was constructed is that each number is the sum of the two numbers to the left in the row or the two numbers below in the column, if there are numbers in these positions. Most numbers can be found by various additions or subtractions of nearby numbers. So, for example, the 17 (in bold above) could be found by $7 + 10$ or $8 + 9$ or $43 - 26$ or perhaps as the sum $4 + 5 + 5 + 3$ (the square of four cells to the bottom left of the 17). Learners will find other more complicated ways as well. There is a rich amount of structure embedded in this grid. (For a spreadsheet that generates values in the cells given four starting numbers, go to www.50maths.com.)

- Imagine the grid continued up and right for ever. It is possible to ask questions about this 'infinite' grid. For example, does 100 appear in this grid? Or 1000? Where? How many times?
- Imagine the grid continued down and left for ever as well. Is −99 in the grid? Where? How many times?

Related Topics
- algebraic expressions
- collecting like terms
- simultaneous equations

Web
A copy of the grid and a related spreadsheet are available at www.50maths. com.

Further Idea
Find out about Leonardo of Pisa (1170–1250), commonly known as Fibonacci, and the Fibonacci sequence of numbers.

- How many numbers do you need to know to complete a grid for as far as you like in every direction? Does it matter where the given numbers are? Are some positions of numbers easier/harder to handle? *You need the values in at least four squares and you need at least two values from at least two different columns or rows.*

There is plenty of opportunity for learners to create puzzles for one another along these lines, some of which can be very difficult to solve. Learners need to be careful with their arithmetic, otherwise the problems may be truly impossible!

The grid above can be seen as being generated from the numbers 2, 3, 1, 4 in the bottom left square of four cells. Starting with letters a, b, c and d in these squares leads to the following general grid:

$2a+3c$	$2b+3d$	$2a+2b+3c+3d$	$2a+4b+3c+6d$	$4a+6b+6c+9d$
$a+2c$	$b+2d$	$a+b+2c+2d$	$a+2b+2c+4d$	$2a+3b+4c+6d$
$a+c$	$b+d$	$a+b+c+d$	$a+2b+c+2d$	$2a+3b+2c+3d$
c	d	$c+d$	$c+2d$	$2c+3d$
a	b	$a+b$	$a+2b$	$2a+3b$

Equating the expressions in particular cells with particular given numbers leads to simultaneous equations, the solution to which provide a, b, c and d.

Extension

- Create different rules about how you get the numbers in each cell. It doesn't have to be 'add the previous two' each time.
- Explore the connections with Fibonacci Sequences.

Fractional Dice

16

Roll two dice and take the smaller number as the numerator and the larger as the denominator of a fraction. (If the two numbers are the same, then it doesn't matter which goes where, as you will just end up with a fraction equal to 1, such as $^3/_3$.)

- What is the probability that you will make a reducible fraction (i.e., one that can be cancelled down)?
- After cancelling, how many different-sized irreducible fractions are possible? What are their probabilities?

A sample space diagram is a convenient approach, leading to the result that there is a probability of $^7/_{18}$ of getting a cancel-down-able fraction (a reducing or simplifying fraction – shown shaded in the table below). There are 12 different possible fractions that can be produced, with probabilities as shown in the table on the next page.

	1	2	3	4	5	6
1	1	$\frac{1}{2}$	$\frac{1}{3}$	$\frac{1}{4}$	$\frac{1}{5}$	$\frac{1}{6}$
2	$\frac{1}{2}$	1	$\frac{2}{3}$	$\frac{1}{2}$	$\frac{2}{5}$	$\frac{1}{3}$
3	$\frac{1}{3}$	$\frac{2}{3}$	1	$\frac{3}{4}$	$\frac{3}{5}$	$\frac{1}{2}$
4	$\frac{1}{4}$	$\frac{1}{2}$	$\frac{3}{4}$	1	$\frac{4}{5}$	$\frac{2}{3}$
5	$\frac{1}{5}$	$\frac{2}{5}$	$\frac{3}{5}$	$\frac{4}{5}$	1	$\frac{5}{6}$
6	$\frac{1}{6}$	$\frac{1}{3}$	$\frac{1}{2}$	$\frac{2}{3}$	$\frac{5}{6}$	1

Ordering the resulting fractions to create the table on the next page is a good exercise to complement work on equivalent fractions, which can otherwise become mechanical and devoid of much awareness of the actual numerical size of the fractions being handled.

Related Topics
- equivalent fractions
- probability

Materials Needed
- ordinary dice
- small stickers

X	$\dfrac{1}{6}$	$\dfrac{1}{5}$	$\dfrac{1}{4}$	$\dfrac{1}{3}$	$\dfrac{2}{5}$	$\dfrac{1}{2}$	$\dfrac{3}{5}$	$\dfrac{2}{3}$	$\dfrac{3}{4}$	$\dfrac{4}{5}$	$\dfrac{5}{6}$	1
$p(X)$	$\dfrac{1}{18}$	$\dfrac{1}{18}$	$\dfrac{1}{18}$	$\dfrac{1}{9}$	$\dfrac{1}{18}$	$\dfrac{1}{6}$	$\dfrac{1}{18}$	$\dfrac{1}{9}$	$\dfrac{1}{18}$	$\dfrac{1}{18}$	$\dfrac{1}{18}$	$\dfrac{1}{6}$

So the most likely values are 1 or ½, each with a probability of ⅙.

Extension

- Having done this work, learners can play *Fraction Bingo*, in which they choose a grid (3 by 3) of simplified fractions (all different). As the dice are thrown, they calculate the fraction and shade it in, and the winner is the first to get three in a row.
- An alternative rule is to multiply the numbers on the two dice, divide by ten and round the result to the nearest integer. The distribution then is:

X	0	1	2	3	4
$p(X)$	$\dfrac{2}{9}$	$\dfrac{15}{16}$	$\dfrac{1}{4}$	$\dfrac{1}{12}$	$\dfrac{1}{36}$

- What other rules can learners invent and analyse with two (or more) dice?
- Using stickers, re-label some dice with fractional quantities. Can you do it so that the probability of the sum being an integer is exactly ½?

Happy Days

17

It is possible to represent qualitative attributes, such as 'happiness', on a graph without assigning numbers to them. (There is a view that maths is always supposed to involve precise quantities, but a task such as this could challenge that.) Sometimes the independent variable might be another qualitative property, but it could be something quantitative, such as time. For example, when you get home from school and someone says 'How was your day?' a mathematician might answer with a graph! So this might be the 'story of my day so far':

Related Topics
• interpreting graphs
• qualitative graphs
• scattergraphs
• travel graphs

Further Idea
Learners might like to find out about 'happiness formulae', such as happiness $= P + 5E + 3H$ (Pete Cohen) or happiness $= H + C + V$ (Martin Seligman) – search the web for more detail – and see whether they think there is anything in them.

Caution
Be prepared for pastoral issues to surface.

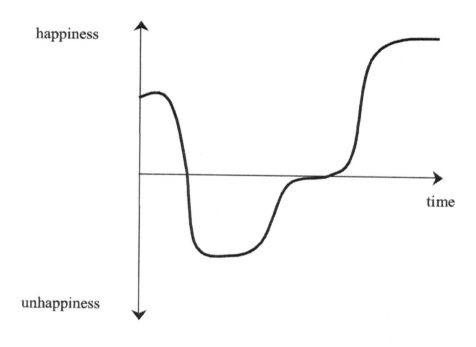

A numerical scale for time may be helpful.

• What was this day like? How would you describe it in words?
• Using a different colour, draw a different day on the same axes. Were the days similar? Why/why not?
• Draw two different people's stories of the same day on the same axes. Do the lines show similarities? Do you think they are in the same class? Are they likely to have much in common with each other? Why?
• Draw a holiday (or a weekend day) and a school day on the same axes. Can someone else identify which was which?

- Add another quantity (e.g., tiredness, interestedness, confusedness, activeness, hungriness, amount of conversation, heaviness of school bag, etc) in a different colour. Which quantities affect each other?

Where two quantities are being considered, a different kind of graph would be possible:

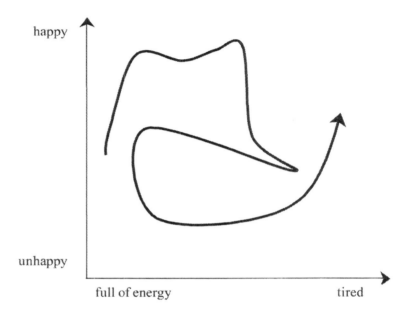

This curve might represent someone's day.

- Can you describe the day in words? Can you account for the shape?

Similar directed curves can be drawn for, say, 'amount of rain' versus 'temperature' for a particular week.

Story time

- On a distance–time graph, illustrate the story of the hare and the tortoise by drawing a curve for each animal. What other well-known stories might it be possible to represent?
- Present an account of a school sports event (a race is easiest) in a graph form rather than as a verbal report. (Perhaps this could feature in an assembly?)

Harshad Numbers

18

Determining mechanically whether arbitrary numbers are divisible by other arbitrary numbers can seem dull and pointless unless something more substantial is going on, so one context to provide some motivation for this sort of work would be to hunt for *Harshad numbers*.

> A *Harshad number* (also known as a *Niven number*) is an integer which is divisible by its digit sum.

(The *digit sum* of a number is — unsurprisingly — the sum of its digits; easily confused with the *digital root*, which is obtained by *repeatedly* digit summing until you are left with a single-digit number.)

Related Topics
- divisibility tests
- factors
- prime numbers

Web
A spreadsheet for generating Harshad numbers is available at www.50maths.com.

- **Find some Harshad numbers. How many can you find in 5 minutes?** *There are 32 Harshad numbers less than 100. All single-digit numbers are Harshad numbers, and the sequence then continues: 10, 12, 18, 20, 21, 24, 27, 30, 36, 40, 42, 45, 48, 50, 54, 60, 63, 70, 72, 80, 81, 84, 90, 100, . . . (See the spreadsheet available at www.50maths. com or the internet for more.)*

- **Which multiples of 9 are Harshad numbers?** *You might think at first that they all would be, since all multiples of 9 (except zero) have a digital root of 9. But because Harshad numbers are concerned with digital sums rather than digital roots some multiples of 9 are not divisible by their digit sums, although of course they would be divisible by their digital roots (9). For example, 99, 189, 279, 369, . . . (multiples of 9 of the form 9(10n + 1) for integer values of n from 1 to 10) are not Harshad numbers.*

- **What is the biggest Harshad number you can find?** *Powers of 10 will clearly be Harshad numbers, since you are just dividing them by 1, so a googol (10^{100}), for instance, will be a big Harshad number.*

- **How many prime numbers are Harshad numbers?** *Four: the only ones are 2, 3, 5 and 7. Any two-or-more-digit prime number will have a sum of digits less than itself but greater than 1, and because it's a prime this number won't go into it.*

- **Were you born in a Harshad year? Is it a Harshad year now? When will the next Harshad year be?** *A relevant portion of the sequence of Harshad numbers is: 1980, 1998, 2000, 2001, 2004, 2007, 2010, 2016, 2020, 2022, 2023, 2024, 2025, 2028, 2030, . . .*

Extension

- Learners could make a graph or chart to investigate and illustrate the distribution of Harshad numbers.
- Learners could define another type of number based on some connection between the digit sum and the number and investigate the properties of their new creation.

I Don't Believe It!

19

Do people understand size and scale? Not always. See what learners make of the claims below. It is not enough just to say 'I don't believe it!' – an atmosphere is needed in which learners seek to convince one another by argument.

You can set this up as a 'circus', with groups of learners moving from claim to claim around the room, writing down whether they agree with the claim and why before moving on to the next one. You could supply useful data centrally or at each station or not at all and require guesstimation exclusively.

- Laurel and Hardy (*The Laurel–Hardy Murder Case* 1930): Stan has just discovered that he may have inherited $3 m. He asks Ollie, 'Say, is that as much as a thousand?' Ollie replies, 'Man alive! It's *twice* as much!' What would you say to them?
- 'It is estimated you can get 50 000 pennies into a cubic foot – a trillion pennies would fill two St Paul's Cathedrals.' (Michael Blastland) *St Paul's Cathedral has a height of 365 feet (easy to remember: the same as the number of days in a year), but the inside has dimensions around 500 feet by 300 feet by 170 feet high, though obviously it is not a cuboid.*
- 'The atomic nucleus in size relative to a whole atom is sometimes compared to a fly in a cathedral.' How accurate is this?
- 'The sizes of moon, earth and sun are sometimes represented by a ball bearing, a tennis ball and a football.' Is this accurate? Can you suggest other more accurately-sized objects? What about the planets in the solar system and their relative sizes and distances? (See below.)
- 'Space isn't remote at all; it's only an hour's drive straight upwards.' (Fred Hoyle) Is he right? *Yes. The Kármán line is at an altitude of 100 km and is often used to define the boundary between the earth's atmosphere and outer space.*
- 'If you took all the human blood in the world, it would fill only a cube 870 feet on each side. Or if you poured it into the Dead Sea it would add only ¾ inch to its height.' True or false? How many Olympic swimming pools would it fill? *An adult contains about 5 litres of blood, an Olympic swimming pool is 25 m × 50 m × 2 m and the surface area of the Dead Sea is about 810 km².*
- 'If you took all the people in the world, you could drop them into a hole 1 km wide by 1 km long by ½ km deep and they would have plenty of room to move about.' *Taking the average volume of a human being as 70 litres and a world population of 6.6 billion gives a total volume of less than 500 million m³, so they should fit easily, provided they didn't mind getting extremely squashed/crushed!*

Related Topics
- dimensions
- estimation
- scale
- units

Materials Needed
- calculators
Print out the claims from www.50maths.com and set them up at stations around the room.

Further Ideas
Cathcart, B. (2005) *The Fly in the Cathedral*, Penguin
Haldane, J. B. S. (1928) *On Being the Right Size*

- 'If you took all the people in the world and gave each one a room 10 m × 10 m × 10 m, you could fit all the rooms into the Grand Canyon.' *True, since the volume of the Grand Canyon is estimated to be around 10^{13} m^3.*
- 'Take a sheet of paper and tear it in half. Put the two pieces together and tear them in half. Put the pieces together and tear them in half, and so on. Assuming you could do it 50 times altogether, the stack would be so high it would be more than halfway to the sun.' *True. It is only about 93 million miles to the sun!*

Extensions

- Conduct a survey to see how accurately people estimate distances. The world is getting smaller all the time with global travel, but do people consequently tend to underestimate distances? (Surveys suggest the opposite.) Questions could include, e.g., 'Which is further: London to Paris or London to Liverpool?' (It might be necessary to agree how much tolerance should be allowed – asking people to distinguish between very similar distances would be unfair.)
- Try drawing a diagram of the solar system to scale. (On typical classroom and textbook pictures, the planets almost overlap each other, but that is massively unrealistic.) Try to indicate relative size and distance. *Don't spend long trying, as learners will discover that they just cannot do this, as the sizes are so hugely different. Failing gives a memorable sense of the scales involved, however.*
- Mass, length, area and volume have been metricated but not time. Invent a system for 'metric time'. How would it work? Would it be convenient? What would be the pros and cons?
- Make up some rhyming mnemonics for measures, like these fairly well-known ones, or try to improve them (e.g., their accuracy):
    - A litre of water's a pint and three-quarters.
    - Two-and-a-fifth pounds of ham weighs about a kilogram.
    - A metre measures three foot three; it's longer than a yard, you see.
- In groups, researching on the internet, learners could make up something memorable for visualizing each power of 10 from, say, 10^2 to 10^{20} (or further); i.e., '10^n is the same as the number of …'. Different groups could deal with different ranges of powers; e.g., 'There are about 10^{19} different states in which you can put a *Rubik's Cube®*'; 'There are about 10^{21} possible 9×9 Sudokus'; 'There are about 10^{68} ways of arranging the cards in a normal pack of 52'.

If A Tree Falls
In A Forest . . .

20

Imagine you are firing a gun in a forest (e.g., paint-balling) where the trees are planted in a regular square array. You could imagine the trees as lattice points on a coordinate grid.

- If you stand at the origin, which trees can you hit and which trees are hidden behind other trees? (Learners could colour them different colours.)
- In what direction(s) would the bullet travel as far as possible?
- If you stand at (a, b), can you make up a rule that says whether you can hit a tree at (c, d)? (You can assume that you are a crack shot and that the bullet will fly absolutely straight until it hits something!) *In fact, you can hit a tree at (c, d) from (a, b) if and only if the fraction*

$$\frac{|d - b|}{|c - a|}$$

is in its lowest terms. This is equivalent to saying that HCF($|d - b|, |c - a|$) = 1.

A different approach to the same task is to take a piece of A4 square-dotty paper and choose any two dots and join them with a straight line.

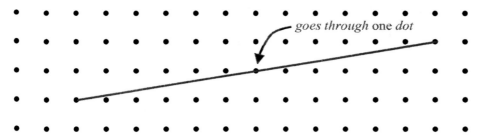

goes through one *dot*

- How many dots (not including the ones at the ends) does the line pass through? The one above goes through 1 dot.
- What is the longest line you can draw that doesn't go through *any* dots?
- If a line *looks* as though it goes close to a dot, but you are not sure whether it goes through exactly or not, can you reason it out?
- How many dots does the line from (0, 0) to (a, b) go through?
- How many dots does the line from (a, b) to (c, d) go through?
- What if a, b, c and d are positive integers? What if they're *not* integers and/or *not* positive? What rules can you discover?

Related Topics
- coordinates
- fractions
- highest common factor (greatest common divisor)

Materials Needed
- long rulers
- square-dotty paper (or ordinary squared paper)

Further Idea
Find out what *Olbers' Paradox* is and relate it to this task.

Caution
If you wish to avoid the metaphor of guns, you can talk about a tree falling down and question whether it hits another tree as it falls or whether it falls in between the surrounding trees. The trees have to be assumed to be infinitely tall and narrow for this to work.

This can be a good task for working with the idea of *highest common factor*, whether learners have met the term explicitly before or not. The question of finding long lines that do not go through any dots involves finding *co-prime* pairs of numbers (numbers with a highest common factor of 1), such as 19 and 28 on a piece of A4 paper.

The difficulty of being sure about diagrams, even when carefully drawn with a sharp pencil and new ruler, may push learners towards reasoning. Pretty soon, learners will start to talk about how far along and up the lines go, so as to justify which trees they will hit and which they won't.

If a, b, c and d are all integers, then the number of dots (not including the end ones) on the line segment joining (a, b) to (c, d) is given by

$$\text{HCF}(|d - b|, |c - a|) - 1.$$

Extensions

- What is the longest line you can draw that goes through exactly 1, 2, 3, … dot(s)?
- How many dots can a circle of radius r and centre (a, b) go through? You will have to make r, a and b non-integer (irrational, even) to get the maximum possible number. (Boomerangs follow an almost circular path, so when you've run out of bullets you could resort to some older technology!) Investigating the number of lattice points *on or inside* a circle of radius r is called the *Gauss Circle Problem*, and has connections with the number π. (The first few numbers, for $r = 0, 1, 2, 3, \ldots$, are 1, 5, 13, 29, 49, 81, …)
- If the forest went on forever in every direction, is there any direction you could fire in and *never* hit a tree? In fact, the answer is that this would be the case for 'most' directions! This surprising result is the consequence of there being 'far more' irrational numbers than rationals.

In The Money

21

- Why are there no 3-pence coins? (There used to be before decimalization in 1971: the 'thrupp'ny bit'.)

  Because 3 is an odd number? But we have 1 pence and 5 pence.

  Because not many things cost 3 pence? But not many things cost *2* pence, either.

If no-one knows, the answer will emerge as learners work on the main task below, but it is to do with 2 and 5 being the prime factors of 10, our decimal number base. It follows from this that amounts based on those numbers are easy to do calculations with.

- If you want to be able to make any amount of money up to £4.99, what's the smallest number of coins you can get away with taking with you? (This may be of *some* practical value if you need to carry coins for machines such as those on buses, although not every value of money is likely to be charged and the machine may not accept every denomination of coin and may perhaps give change.)

Initially, people often assume that you need 499 pennies, but on more thought this often changes to one penny and 249 2-pence coins. It is probably easier to start by deciding how you are going to make 1 pence, 2 pence, 3 pence, and so on. Clear logical thinking is necessary.

The answer with UK currency (other currencies, such as Euros and Australian dollars, work in the same denominations) is:

To make up to 4p	you need	1p (2), 2p (1)
To make up to 9p	you need	1p (2), 2p (1), 5p (1)
To make up to 19p	you need	1p (2), 2p (1), 5p (1), 10p (1)
To make up to 49p	you need	1p (2), 2p (1), 5p (1), 10p (2), 20p (1)
To make up to 99p	you need	1p (2), 2p (1), 5p (1), 10p (2), 20p (1), 50p (1)
To make up to £4.99	you need	1p (2), 2p (1), 5p (1), 10p (2), 20p (1), 50p (1), £1 (2), £2 (1)

(From 4p upwards, you could swap one of your two 1p coins for a 2p and make 1p more with the same number of coins.)

Related Topics
- money
- place value

Web
Coin statistics are readily available on the web, if you need data such as size and weight: www.royalmint.com/RoyalMint/web/site/Corporate/Corp_british_coinage/CurrentSpecifications.asp.

Learners might choose to work in column headings like hundreds-tens-units, using the coin values from right to left:

£2	£1	50	20	10	5	2	1		value
							1	=	1
						1	0	=	2
						1	1	=	3
						1	2	=	4
					1	0	0	=	5
					1	0	1	=	6
					1	1	0	=	7
					1	1	1	=	8
					1	1	2	=	9
				1	0	0	0	=	10
				1	0	0	1	=	11
				1	0	1	0	=	12
				1	0	1	1	=	13
				1	0	1	2	=	14
				1	1	0	0	=	15
				1	1	0	1	=	16
				1	1	1	0	=	17
				1	1	1	1	=	18
				1	1	1	2	=	19

… and so on.

Sometimes you have a choice; e.g., with amounts like 7p, you can have either 5p + 2p or 5p + 1p + 1p. The vertical patterns in this table are also interesting to study.

Banknotes continue to go up in the same numbers, except that in England there is no £100 note (although there is in Northern Ireland and Scotland).

- What difference does it make if you want to minimize the total *value* of the coins needed, rather than the total *number* of them? What about minimizing the total *mass*?

Extensions

- The US system is quite different. Half-dollar (50¢) and dollar (100¢) coins are rarely used, the main coins in circulation being: 1¢ (penny), 5¢ (nickel), 10¢ (dime) and 25¢ (quarter). Learners could look at how to make up different amounts with the minimum number of these coins.
- Can you design a currency that works better than any of these ones?
- With lots of shop prices being 'so-many-pounds and 99 pence', some people are calling for the introduction of a 99p coin. (It is claimed that a lot of time is wasted by everybody waiting for their 1-pence change.) What do you think about this?

In The Money Again

22

The table of data on the right could provide an interesting start.

* What do you notice about the numbers in this table?

coin	mass (g)
£2	12.0
£1	9.5
50p	8.0
20p	5.0
10p	6.5
5p	3.25
2p	7.12
1p	3.56

© www.royalmint.com

Typical observations might include some of the following:

* all the masses are low, for convenience and economy of production;
* generally the more valuable coins are heavier, but the 2p and the 10p are out of line;
* the 2p weighs twice as much as the 1p, and the 10p weighs twice as much as the 5p, but those are the only cases where the mass is proportional to the value. So you could weigh a mixed bag of coppers (1p's and 2p's), for example, divide by 3.56, and that would be the total amount of money. And you could do something similar for 5p's and 10p's. A scatter diagram of value against mass might be useful.

* Suppose a handful of coins weighs 23.25 g. What coins could there be? What would be the total value? *The answer is 20p (4) and 5p (1).* Is there only one possibility? How do you know?
* Could you design a rule so that you could weigh a handful of coins on a very accurate balance and then somehow convert the weight into the value of the coins? What conditions would you need to impose (e.g., which values of coins might be present) so that the machine couldn't be fooled? *This question relates to lowest common multiples.*
* If you could choose the masses of the coins, how much would you decide that each one should weigh so that you could more easily determine the total value of a pile of coins? (A proportional system would be easiest, where £1 has a mass 100 times that of 1p, although this would have a lot of practical problems.)
* What if you wanted to be able to tell the *exact numbers* of each coin present? Could you do it just by weighing the whole pile?

Related Topics

* binary numbers
* lowest common multiples
* place value
* proportionality
* scattergraphs

In fact, you could if you used the masses in the table on the right for instance:

Here, every mass corresponds to one and only one possible collection of coins; e.g., $51 = 32 + 16 + 2 + 1 = 110011$ in binary, so 51 g would correspond to $50p + 20p + 2p + 1p = 73p$; there is no other way of making 51 from these values. There is much to investigate here.

coin	mass (g)
£2	128
£1	64
50p	32
20p	16
10p	8
5p	4
2p	2
1p	1

Web

Coin statistics are readily available on the web, if you need facts such as size and weight: www. royalmint.com/RoyalMint/ web/site/Corporate/ Corp_british_coinage/ CurrentSpecifications.asp.

The Counterfeit Coins

You have 10 sacks of gold coins. In each sack, all the coins are identical, and there are a lot of coins in each sack. However, the coins in one of the sacks are *all* counterfeit and weigh 1 g less than they should. You know how much the coins should weigh, and you have an accurate balance, but you are allowed *only one weighing* to find which is the dodgy sack. How do you do it?

One answer is to take 1 coin from sack 1, 2 coins from sack 2, 3 coins from sack 3, 4 coins from sack 4, and so on (taking one more coin each time) and place the whole pile on the balance. You will have taken 55 coins altogether (the 10th triangle number), so if the reading is 1 g under (1 g less than it should be if all 55 coins were genuine), then the dodgy sack is the first sack; if the reading is 2 g less than it should be, then the dodgy sack is the second sack, and so on.

Extensions

- If you have an unlimited supply of 2p and 5p coins only, which amounts of money can you make and which can't you? For example, you can make 12p by using $2p + 5p + 5p$. Investigate.
- What if you have 5p and 10p coins only instead?

The answer is that with 2p and 5p coins you can make 2 pence (obviously) and any amount greater than 3 pence. In general, with a-pence and b-pence coins (where a and b are co-prime), the highest amount you *cannot* make is $ab - a - b$. With 5p and 10p coins, you can make only multiples of 5p, since the coin values are *not* co-prime.

It's Snowing!

23

It can be fun to start a lesson on reflection by writing some instructions on the board like this. Pupils can usually read it fairly easily.

This can be a good lesson to save for when it snows. Pupils get excited and it may be useful to have something up your sleeve that exploits the circumstances a bit. It is also not the end of the world if pupils who don't make it into school that day miss it!

From a young age, learners will have folded circles of paper into sixths, cut pieces out and unfolded to make snowflake designs. However, producing the same design without folding or cutting – merely by drawing – can be quite challenging. Reflecting in six mirror lines arranged at 60° to one another can be tricky, especially if you choose a difficult design to begin with. Guidance from the teacher can lead to good differentiation with this task.

On A4 isometric paper, draw a regular hexagon with side lengths 10 cm. (This fits on well, even if the paper has a border.) Put in the three diagonals by joining opposite vertices. Then join the mid-points of opposite edges. (Some people find this easier if they first measure 5 cm along each side and put a mark.) Then you are ready. Choose one of your 12 right-angled triangles and draw in any design you like that you can make by joining dot to dot with a pencil and ruler. Then reflect this design in the neighbouring mirror lines, and keep on reflecting what you have so far in the remaining lines, until you have your finished snowflake:

Related Topic
- reflection symmetry

Materials Needed
- A4 isometric paper
- mirrors (possibly)
- snow outside (if possible!)

Web
It is possible to use a beautiful website such as www.its.caltech. edu/~atomic/snowcrystals/ photos/photos.htm for inspiration. And you can make a snowflake pattern quite quickly using http:// gwydir.demon.co.uk/jo/ symmetry/snow.htm.

Further Idea
Stewart, I. (2001) *What Shape Is a Snowflake?*, Freeman.

Extensions

- Obviously you can always do another one, perhaps with a more intricate design. It is easy, if you wish, to justify *not* allowing pupils to colour them in when they inevitably ask (You can just ask them, 'What colour are snowflakes?')!

- The finished drawings can provoke some interesting questions regarding symmetry; e.g., Do snowflakes always have both order 6 rotational symmetry and 6 lines of symmetry? Can you invent a shape which has one of these properties but not the other? *The answers are that the idealized snowflake does have both line and rotational symmetry. Six lines of symmetry implies order 6 rotational symmetry, but the reverse is not true: if you arrange six identical unsymmetrical flags, say, at 60° to each other from a point, like a fan, the resulting shape will have order 6 rotational symmetry but no lines of symmetry.* How many lines of symmetry are possible given order 6 rotational symmetry? *The answer is 0 or 6 only.*

- Looking for less obvious signs of symmetry in the world around us can be a good homework. (Take a picture of it with your mobile phone?) Find … an object with more than order 8 rotational symmetry (perhaps excluding circles) … an object with rotational symmetry but no lines of symmetry … It doesn't have to be just physical objects; one example of musical symmetry might be the 'Crab Canon', J. S. Bach.

Lattice-Point Triangles

24

There are 49 (7^2) integer coordinate points (lattice points) on the grid on the right.

Choose three points (three different learners might choose them) and join them to make a triangle. (If the three points lie on a straight line, it might be simpler to change one of them for the present, although noting helpfully for later that this can happen.)

For example, (1, 2), (3, 6) and (5, 4).

- What kind of triangle is it? *This one is acute-angled isosceles.*
- Work out the area of the triangle. This could be done by dividing it into triangles and/or rectangles, but it is usually easier to enclose the triangle in the smallest possible rectangle and subtract the unnecessary triangles from round the edge, as shown at the bottom right:

Area of triangle $= 4 \times 4 - 4 - 4 - 2 = 6$ cm²

- Draw some more triangles with an area of exactly 6 cm² (or whatever it comes to).

Clearly, learners can draw congruent triangles in other positions and orientations, and some good exhaustive thinking is necessary to find all the possible positions. Then learners will need to step out into *non-congruent* triangles with the same area. It might be natural to begin with right-angled triangles.

- Try to find a connection between the coordinates and the area, so that you can calculate the area of the triangle without drawing or visualizing it at all.

For coordinates (a, b), (c, d) and (e, f), the area of the triangle formed may be written as the absolute value of

$$\frac{1}{2} \begin{vmatrix} c-a & e-a \\ d-b & f-b \end{vmatrix}, \quad \text{or} \quad \frac{1}{2} |(a-c)(b-f)-(a-e)(b-d)|.$$

(General results are easier to find if certain of the values of a to f are set at zero – points on axes.)

- What does it mean when this expression equals zero? *The points must be collinear – on a straight line.*

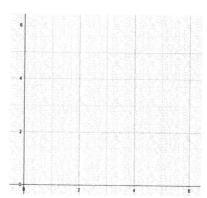

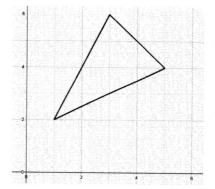

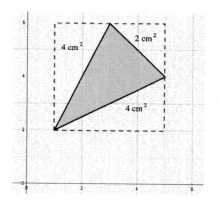

Related Topics
- area
- coordinates

Web

A spreadsheet calculator for this task is available at www.50maths.com.

Further Ideas

Find out what *Pick's Theorem* is and how it relates to this task.

Older pupils who have come across vectors might like to look into the *vector cross-product*.

Extensions

- Working with *quadrilaterals* is harder, because the order in which you state the vertices matters. (Are you going in order round the edge or jumping across the middle?) You can treat a quadrilateral as two triangles glued together, and so although it is more complicated it isn't necessarily that much harder. One way to tell whether your coordinates have been given cyclically is to find the area of the quadrilateral twice, by splitting the shape along what you suppose to be the two different 'diagonals', and check that the answers come out the same.

- Look at perimeters. This is probably worth doing only if learners are familiar with Pythagoras' Theorem.

Logarithmic Spirals

25

This is a way of practising the techniques involved in enlargement as a collaborative task.

Give everyone the same starting shape on the right. (This is available at www.50 maths.com for use on the board or for photocopying onto paper.)

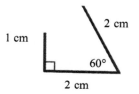

The idea is for different learners to enlarge it by different scale factors. Suitable scale factors of enlargement are 2, 4, 8 and 16. Note that you will need A3 paper for a 16 × enlargement. Other possible scale factors are ½ and ¼, but these can be fiddly. There is much scope for differentiation here, with early finishers doing more awkward enlargements that fit in between those being produced by others.

Possible methods to use would include:

- Measure the angles with a protractor and the sides with a ruler, multiply the side lengths by the scale factor (but don't multiply the angles!) and draw the enlargement. (It would be possible to construct the 60° and 90° angles using compasses rather than a protractor if preferred.)
- Glue, trace or draw the starting shape into a sensible position on the paper and carefully choose a good location for the centre of enlargement. Draw rays from the centre of enlargement and measure along the rays to construct the image. Check afterwards with a protractor that the angles have been preserved and measure the side lengths of the image to ensure that they are the scale factor multiple of the original ones.
- Place a grid over the starting shape and copy each bit onto a larger grid.

Different learners could use different methods and compare afterwards with regard to speed, accuracy, ease, etc.

You could minimize waste of paper by asking learners to plan in rough and do calculations to ensure that their images will fit on the paper they are using. Learners could work in groups so that all those doing enlargement by the same scale factor are working together on one table (a *big* table in some cases, or perhaps the floor).

Once most of the enlarging is complete, the groups need to be re-sorted so that you end up with groups each containing six (say) learners with six different enlargements. Then lay out the enlargements in order in each group, fit them

If you would prefer learners to construct the starting shape for themselves, the necessary information is given below:

Construct the three lines shown above and then join it up at the top.

Related Topic
- enlargement

Materials Needed
- calculators
- long rulers and metre sticks
- paper of various sizes
- protractors and maybe compasses
- starting shape
- tracing paper

Web
For a copy of the starting shape used in this lesson, go to www.50maths.com.

Further Idea

Find out where and why *logarithmic spirals* (also called *equiangular spirals* or *growth spirals*) occur in nature.

together (as shown below) and glue them down onto backing paper. The beginning of the result is shown below:

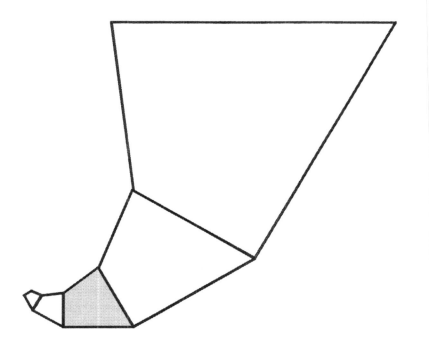

Since the pieces should fit together exactly, there is an element of checking. If somebody's piece is wrong, it will need adjusting or redrawing by the group.

Questions for Plenary Reflection

- What do you see in the final assembled picture?
- What was it about the original shape that made the enlargements fit together at the end in the way that they did? Can you construct a different shape that will work? What different scale factors might be possible? *It isn't very difficult to produce suitable starting shapes – you just need two non-parallel non-adjacent sides such that one is k times the length of the other (e.g., 2 cm and 1 cm in the above shape). Then your scale factors are k^n, where n takes values such as 1, 2, 3, and –1, –2, etc.*

The result is an approximation to a *logarithmic spiral*, a commonly-occurring spiral in nature. This method of construction suggests why these are so prevalent in the biological world: parts of an organism grow, then a new portion starts growing adjacent to the previous one, and so on.

Extension

Learners may become aware as they work on this task that a 'four times' enlargement is much more than 'four times' bigger; i.e., that area scale factor is the square of linear scale factor, so a 'four times enlargement' drawing has 16 times as much area.

Macfarlane's Law

26

This is named after Canadian journalist David Macfarlane (b. 1952) and states:

You can talk faster than you can type, but you can read faster than you can listen.

So, to communicate a message to someone, it saves the *sender* time if they speak it (e.g., by using the telephone) but it saves the *recipient* time if they type it (e.g., by sending an email). So there is potentially a conflict regarding what is the best means of communication. (The fact that reading speed generally exceeds speaking speed is obvious when watching a subtitled film.)

Learners might agree or disagree with this, but it is the sort of thing that might fairly easily be tried out on whoever you have available. Issues to consider might include:

- Are we going to average these speeds across all the people in our sample or look at whether particular individuals can do one thing quicker than another?
- What would constitute a 'fair' test? What sort of text would it be sensible to use?
- Are teenagers likely to be slower/faster at any of these than adults? (For example, faster typers and speakers but slower readers, possibly?)
- Would office workers who use these skills in their jobs be significantly faster than school pupils?
- You might need to find someone who can speak quickly in order not to limit listening speed by speaking speed.
- Does 'reading' mean 'with comprehension' and how will you judge that?

Related Topics

- designing statistical experiments
- handling data
- making and testing statistical hypotheses

Materials Needed

- computers
- reading matter
- stopwatches (from the science or PE departments, perhaps)
- tape recorders (possibly)

The standard 'words per minute' definition in common use is that a 'word' is five key-strokes long, so 'mathematics', for instance, would count as two words. With that definition, typical adult values might be as shown on the right:

Learners can devise practical methods for investigating this, and then on computers use whatever statistical techniques they have to process their data – at its simplest, calculating and comparing averages.

mode	typical speeds (words per minute)
typing	60–80
speaking	150–200
listening	200–250
reading	250–300

Discussion

- Will knowing your own 'rates' affect how you do things in the future? Will it motivate you to work at increasing your typing speed, for instance?

- What do you think about the dilemma implied by the Law as stated?
- Speed isn't everything; what other factors are relevant? (For example, ability to interact/interrupt, etc on the telephone, ability to save a copy on email, etc.)
- What about handwriting speed? (Typically 20–30 words per minute.) Can you write faster than you can type? Should you be allowed to use word-processors in exams?

Extensions

Learners may have ideas of other everyday human activities that they could investigate statistically. For example,

- Is it true that the higher the ratio of ring finger length to index finger length, the more 'sporty' a person is? Are there male/female differences? How similar is the ratio on a person's left and right hands? (A study that looked into this question was run by Tim Spector, King's College London – there are lots of links on the web.)

Meanness

27

How *mean* are you? Who's the *meanest* person in the room? Assign A = 1, B = 2, etc, and add up the values for the letters in your first name. Divide by the number of letters to obtain a 'mean value'; e.g.,

$$\text{'David'} = \frac{4+1+22+9+4}{5} = 8,$$

and that is his 'meanness'.

- How 'mean' is your surname/middle name?
- Is the mean of your first name and your surname the same as the mean of your whole name? *Not necessarily; only if the means of the first name and surname are the same or if the lengths of the names are the same.*
- How mean is your teacher/year head/head teacher?
- Are David and Liam meaner separately or when combined?!
- Make a meanness scale for the class.
- What is the meanest animal? Is a lion meaner than a monkey?

This sort of task encourages learners to notice what happens to the mean when you combine two sets of values. David (8) Clark (9) is DavidClark (8.5), and 8.5 is the mean of 8 and 9, but David (8) Clarkson (11.625) is DavidClarkson (10.23 . . .), and 10.23 . . . is bigger than 9.8125 (the mean of 8 and 11.625). This happens because the surname (with the bigger mean) is longer than the first name, so contributes a bigger weight to the overall mean. Learners can investigate the effect of adding 'Mr' or 'Ms', etc, to the front of their names. Will the mean go up or down?

Extensions

- Using a different code for the letters of the alphabet doesn't offer many new possibilities but may be helpful for making it clear to learners that A doesn't *have* to equal 1 just because it is the first letter of the alphabet – a common misconception that may be exacerbated by this sort of task if you are not careful.
- You could offer the idea of a *geometric* mean (*multiply* the values of the letters and take the *nth root* of the answer, where n is the number of letters). Learners could research other kinds of mean, such as the 'harmonic mean' or invent their own definition.

Related Topic
- averages

Web

A program called *AlphabetCalculator* is available at www.50maths.com to make light work of these calculations. This can be useful for plenary discussions or for marking learners' work.

If you have a first name of length n_f and mean x_f and a surname of length n_s and mean x_s, the overall mean of both names will be

$$\frac{n_f x_f + n_s x_s}{n_f + n_s};$$

for a middle name as well, using the same labels, the overall mean will be

$$\frac{n_f x_f + n_m x_m + n_s x_s}{n_f + n_m + n_s},$$

and so on.

Alphametics

A slightly-related activity could be for pupils to construct alphametics based on one another's names; e.g.

```
  RAVIN
  SUNNY
+  GUY
  ─────
  ARGUE
  ─────
```

Each letter stands for one and only one digit (0 to 9), and the first letters of each number cannot be zero. The best ones, like this one, have exactly one solution. Learners will often work for much longer and with far greater enthusiasm on tasks related to their own or one another's names than they might on less 'personalized' exercises.

Ninety-Nine Zillion Gazillion

Ask learners to put up their hands and say 'a big number'. Words such as 'million', 'billion', 'trillion' and sometimes 'zillion' (and their multiples) are common answers, with pupils often trying to outdo the last answer by going bigger, perhaps by using lots of nines (or saying 'plus one'!). Someone may have heard of a googol or a googolplex, and if you get 'infinity' you could debate whether that is really 'a number'.

Discuss how many zeroes these numbers have. (Zillion is not a mathematically-defined quantity – it just means 'quite a lot'!) Although learners may know how to write such big numbers in digits, they may not have much sense of their size. So draw a horizontal number line on the board and put zero at the left end and 'a billion' (written perhaps just as 'b', so it doesn't take up too much room) at the right end:

```
0                                                    b
```

Then ask learners to come to the board and mark with an 'm', as accurately as they can, where they think 'a million' ought to go. Answers tend to vary wildly. Then in groups, or as a whole class, try to justify or criticize the various locations; e.g.,

- 'A million is, like, loads, so it must be down the billion end.'
- 'Compared with a billion, a million is quite small, but compared with nothing it's quite big, so I think it goes in the middle.'
- 'I think it could be basically anywhere along there but not too near the ends.'

If an incorrect consensus is reached, it can usually be disturbed by asking where 'two million' would be, and the discussion then takes off again. Even those who realize that a million belongs nearer the left end than the right end are often surprised when they eventually reason that, if the number line is 1 metre long, a million belongs only 1 mm from the left end, since 1000 million = 1 billion. It is then interesting to imagine where 'a trillion' would come on the line: 1 kilometre away – in the middle of town, perhaps. This can be an interesting point when you consider how similar '£2 m' and '£2 b' sound to the average newspaper reader!

Related Topics
- estimation
- powers of 10
- standard form

Web
Watch http://micro.magnet.fsu.edu/primer/java/science opticsu/powersof10/ – this is actually quite awe-inspiring.

Further Ideas
Learners could find out about *Graham's number* and *Skewe's number* or research the definitions of googol, googolplex, milliard, centillion, lakh, crore, millillion, etc.

This task obviously assumes a linear rather than a logarithmic number line, and this may be worth considering, since learners may have met logarithmic scales (although not, perhaps, the name) in science (e.g., electromagnetic spectrum, Richter scale, decibels, pitch in music) and they will also have met non-linear schematic number lines as timelines in history (geological timelines are sometimes logarithmic), as well as the 'empty number line' in maths, in which case the answer below may be reasonable:

So if learners place 'million' two-thirds of the way along, this may have something to do with it, since the progression along column headings for base-ten numbers (Th, H, T, U, t, h, etc) is a logarithmic scale.

Extensions

- Say something that costs about a million/billion/trillion pounds.
- How long would it take you to write all the numbers up to a million/billion/googol? (Think about how many 1-digit, 2-digit, etc, numbers there will be.)
- What was happening a million/billion/trillion seconds/minutes/hours ago? (Learners could make up true/false questions for one another such as 'Western civilization has not been around for a trillion seconds'.)

	hours	minutes	seconds
million	Just over 100 years. What things were being invented 100 years ago?	About 2 years.	About 12 days.
billion	About 100 million years. 100 million years ago, the earth was in the middle of the Cretaceous period; dinosaurs were roaming around.	About 1900 years ago, so just into the second century CE. Who was alive then?	About 32 years. Were your parents alive then? Your teacher? What kind of cars were being driven? What clothes were being worn? Who was Prime Minister?
trillion	About 100 billion years. This is a problem, since the consensus among scientists is that the universe is (only!) about 13.7 billion years old, so there would be no such time.	About 2 million years ago *Homo erectus* (upright human beings who would look similar to us but had smaller brains and more ape-like features) were wandering around in Africa.	About 32 000 years. *Homo sapiens* were doing well.

Odd One Out

29

Which of these numbers is equal to the mean of the other four?

2, 4, 7, 9, 13 *The answer is 7.*

Related Topics
• averages and range

Web
A spreadsheet that calculates mean, median, mode and range is available at www.50maths.com.

Learners may initially approach this by working out the mean of each possible group of four (which may lead to some useful calculating practice). However, an easier way is simply to find the mean of all five numbers. If you have a set of four numbers and you add an extra number equal to the value of their mean, it will not change the overall mean: you can add as many 7s to this list as you like, and the mean will never change. This is often a surprise to learners, but is fundamentally related to what a mean is, and tends to emerge from this task after answering a few questions of this kind.

- Can the answer ever be the highest/lowest number in the set? *Not unless all the numbers are the same.*
- Is it always the middle number? *No; e.g., the answer for 3, 3, 4, 5, 10 is 5.*

Asking learners to make up questions like this (an 'easy', 'medium' and 'hard' version) can lead to good thinking, as they will probably want all the numbers to be integers and they may not initially find this easy. (The mean will stick out if there is only one non-integer, since in that case it has to be the mean. However, if you have *two* non-integers in the list, one or neither can be the mean; e.g., the answer for 2, 3½ , 6, 7, 11½ is 6, an integer.)

- Which of these numbers is equal to the *mode* of the other four?
  2, 3, 3, 3, 8 *The answer is 3.*
- This question type is rather easy. Why? *Adding a number equal to the mode just makes that number even more the mode than it was before – it is even more obviously the answer.*
- Which of these numbers is equal to the *median* of the other four?
  3, 4, 7, 10, 13 *The answer is 7.*
- Must the answer always be the median of the *five* numbers? *Yes.* Why? *Adding a number at precisely the middle point of a set of data cannot shift the middle either up or down but must leave it where it is.*

Finally,

- Which of these numbers is equal to the *range* of the other four?
  3, 4, 7, 10, 13 *The answer is 10.*

- Must the answer always be the range of the *five* numbers? *No.*
- Make up an example where the answer is *not* equal to the range of the five numbers. *For example, 3, 10, 11, 12, 13; where the answer is either 3 or 10 (3 in this case).*
- Make up an example where there is *only one answer* and it is *not* equal to the range of the five numbers. *This is possible only if you allow at least one negative number; e.g., −2, 1, 3, 8, 10; where the answer is 10.*

After learners have obtained some sense of what is possible and impossible in this setting, groups or individuals can work on writing questions for one another, based on giving conditions on (some of) the mean, median, mode, range and number of values, and requiring a list of possible values as the answer. Answerers might seek to provide all possible solutions or to prove that a solution is impossible; questioners might seek to construct problems that have exactly one solution.

Possible prompts might be:

- Write an easy/medium/hard question.
- Write an impossible question.
- Write an impossible question that is not *obviously* impossible.
- Write a *possible* question that *looks* impossible.

One Of Our Vertices Is Missing!

30

You are given the points (2, 1) and (3, 2), say. Which two other points are needed, along with these, to make a square?

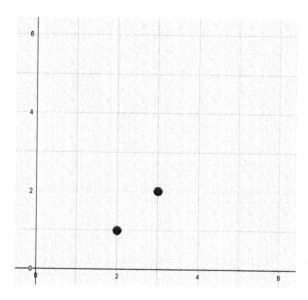

Related Topics

- gradient
- quadrilaterals
- vectors

Web

For a spreadsheet that generates the required coordinates, go to www.50maths.com.

Further Idea

Learners might like to find out about the game Quod, invented by Keith Still, and try playing it. There are interactive versions on the web, or see Stewart, I. (2006) *How to Cut a Cake*, OUP, page 71.

- Given the coordinates of *two* points, is it *always* possible to find two more points such that the four points together are the vertices of a square?
- Is it sometimes/always/never possible to find more than one solution? What if the coordinates have to be integers?
- Can you invent a rule for finding the other two points without having to do a drawing?
- Can you extend this problem to other quadrilaterals? How many points do you have to begin with?
- Can you extend this problem to other polygons? What conditions do you need?

The problem, as stated, does not require the two given points to be adjacent – they could be diagonal. If (2, 1) and (3, 2) are *diagonal* points, then (2, 2) and (3, 1) must be the remaining two. Otherwise, if (2, 1) and (3, 2) are *adjacent* points, then there are two possibilities for the remaining pair: either (3, 0) and (4, 1) or (1, 2) and (2, 3). So altogether there are three possibilities here, and in each case the coordinates are all integers.

This task is intended to lead to some drawing of squares (normal and tilted) and consideration of the slopes of the sides. By considering the displacement vectors along each side (not necessarily formally – learners do not need to have officially 'met' vectors), for specific coordinate values, it may be possible to arrive at conjectures regarding the relationships between the coordinates at each vertex.

A complete generalization would be something like the following:

If (a, b) and (c, d) are *adjacent* points on a square, the other two points must be given by $(c + d - b, a + d - c)$ and $(a + d - b, a + b - c)$ or $(b + c - d, c + d - a)$ and $(a + b - d, b + c - a)$.

If (a, b) and (c, d) are *diagonal* points on a square, the other two points must be given by $(\frac{1}{2}(a + b + c - d), \frac{1}{2}(b + c + d - a))$ and $(\frac{1}{2}(a + c + d - b), \frac{1}{2}(a + b + d - c))$.

A spreadsheet which calculates these positions given a, b, c and d is available at www.50maths.com.

For any other type of quadrilateral, more than two starting points will be necessary, in order to avoid an infinity of solutions.

Given the starting points (a, b), (c, d) and (e, f), as three vertices of a *rectangle*, in cyclic order, there is only one possibility for the fourth: it must be at $(a + e - c, b + f - d)$. (To verify that the point (c, d) is adjacent to the two others, check that $(b - d)(d - f) = (a - c)(e - c)$.)

Given the starting points (a, b), (c, d) and (e, f), as three vertices of a *parallelogram*, without knowing anything else, there are three possibilities for the third vertex: $(a + e - c, b + f - d)$, $(c + e - a, d + f - b)$ or $(a + c - e, b + d - f)$ – see below:

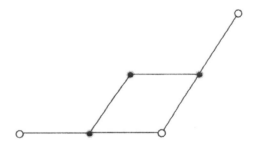

The filled dots are the given three vertices of the parallelogram and the empty dots indicate the three possible positions for the final vertex.

Extensions

It is inviting to pursue other quadrilaterals, and lot of interesting work can follow. The aim is not necessarily to reach the complicated generalizations above but to find some relationships and the bounds of possibility once certain constraints are accepted.

One Straight Cut

31

Take a piece of A4 paper (or a sheet of newspaper if you are demonstrating to a whole class), fold it in half and in half again and cut off (in a straight line) the corner that came from the centre of the page (where the two fold lines meet):

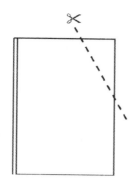

Unfold the paper.

- What shape hole do you get in the centre?
- Depending on the angle of your cut, what shapes are possible?

You will always get a rhombus, because the cut line determines the length of the sides and this must be the same for all four sides. The rhombus will be a square if you cut at 45° to the sides.

- What can you change about this to ask some more questions?

One possibility is to keep the 'one straight cut' rule but to change the way the paper is folded up. If you initially fold the paper in half but then fold the second fold at an angle, what shapes can you get from this by one straight cut? Can you get a rhombus?

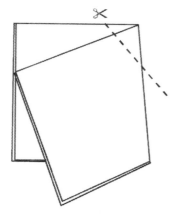

Here, all you can get is a kite or, if you cut perpendicular to the second paper fold line, an isosceles triangle.

- What determines what *kind* of isosceles triangle you get? *The answer is the angle of the second fold.*

It is good to encourage learners to work on their visual imagery before actually trying it, and to try to think of all the possibilities in advance.

There are lots of ways of extending this task by changing the number or direction of the folds and perhaps by allowing a continuous cut along *two* straight lines (i.e., one change of direction mid-cut). A lot of clear thinking about reflection symmetry is necessary.

Extensions

- A possible puzzle that learners can devise is 'Which one of these is the odd one out?', followed by drawings of five, say, opened-out pieces of paper, four of which were produced by folding and cutting in some specified way and one of which is a plausible impostor that could not have been made in that fashion.
- Take a rectangle and make one straight cut with a pair of scissors so that you end up with two pieces. What possible shapes can the pieces be? Try to consider all possible situations. *You can get 2 rectangles (congruent or not), 2 right-angled trapeziums (congruent or not), 2 congruent right-angled triangles, 1 (possibly isosceles) right-angled triangle and 1 right-angled trapezium, 1 right-angled triangle (possibly isosceles) and 1 right-angled pentagon.*

One Thousand Dice

32

How much would it cost to send one thousand dice through the post? (I have no idea why you would want to! This is intended as a problem-solving task, not a contrived real-life scenario.) The mass of the dice can be estimated or measured (you could weigh them in advance if you will not have access to a balance during the lesson).

Questions to consider might include:

- If all the dice are identical, what is the best way to find the mass of one of them? (Perhaps weigh 10 and divide by 10?) Measuring the side lengths should be straightforward, but are the dice exactly cubic?
- What arrangement of the dice will be most economical? What sizes and shapes of parcel are allowed by the postal regulations? Do you want a $10 \times 10 \times 10$ cube or a $1 \times 10 \times 100$ sheet or something else? There will be both mass and size restrictions.
- Might it be necessary/better to make up two or more smaller packages rather than one big one? What factors do you need to consider? *Cost, allowable shapes/sizes, maximum allowable mass, ease of carrying, sturdiness for transit, fitting through a letterbox / post-box? etc.*
- What about the packaging? Which shape of parcel(s) will require the least paper and tape? Will some shapes of package need reinforcing cardboard? Will some be able to maintain their own shape without it?

Dice are convenient for this because they are readily available in maths departments and their cube shape simplifies volume calculations. Since they are quite small, you can consider quite a large number (1000), leading to lots of possible arrangements. Setting pupils to work in groups to see which group can post the dice for the least cost can be fun.

It is good to encourage visualization and calculation rather than just measurement, and it is very unlikely that you will have enough dice for any group to have 1000.

Extensions

- Matchboxes are a good deal more complicated, since being cuboids rather than cubes they can be put together in different orientations. Perhaps considering just 24 matchboxes and the possible cuboid shapes into

Related Topics
- surface area
- volume

Materials Needed
- A3 or bigger scrap paper for wrapping up
- a few dice (you don't need 1000 of them!)
- calculators
- free leaflets or printouts of information from www. royalmail.com
- possibly an accurate balance from the science department
- rulers

Further Ideas
Learners might be interested in finding out about sphere packing problems, 'kissing number' and applications to the structure of crystals.

which they could be packed would be a sensible start. The dimensions of a matchbox might be taken as 1.5 cm × 3 cm × 6 cm.

- A related problem is packing a collection of dice or matchboxes into a bigger cuboid box of specified size. Learners can work out the percentage of space filled/wasted.

One-Hundred-And-Ten Per Cent

33

Present the flow chart below (a copy is available at www.50maths.com). At each point, calculations are done based on the amount present *at that stage*.

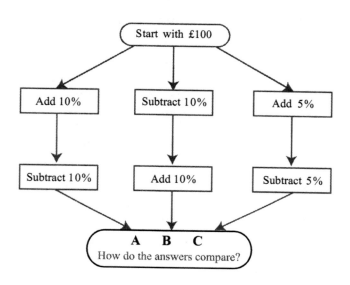

Related Topics
• money calculations
• percentage increase and decrease

Materials Needed
• calculators
• the starting flow chart

Web
For a copy of the flow chart and of the table of percentage changes, go to www.50maths.com.

Before learners work on this in groups or individually, you could take predictions (a vote?) on what will happen. Will the answers all be the same? Will one be higher than the others? Which amount – A, B or C – would you choose to have?

If the calculations are done correctly, then there are likely to be some surprises. A and B lead to the same result, but not £100, since $100 \times 1.1 \times 0.9 = 100 \times 0.9 \times 1.1 = £99$. Where has the missing pound gone? C is *slightly* higher: $100 \times 1.05 \times 0.95 = £99.75$. Trying to express what is going on in words can be very useful but hard. The 10% you take off in A is a little larger than the 10% you added on just before, because the 10% you take off is 10% of a larger amount (£110). Diagrams such as the following may help:

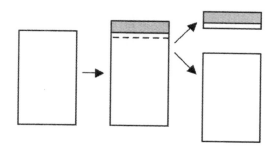

It might seem frustrating that whichever way round you do it you always seem to lose money! (Perhaps this relates to such observations as *Murphy's Law*.)

Learners could make posters to explain what is happening. Further avenues to explore would be:

- Generalize to any starting amount of money (*a*). *A = B = 0.99a; C = 0.9975a.*
- Generalize to any equal percentage increase and decrease (*p*%).

$$A = B = \left(1 + \frac{p}{100}\right)\left(1 - \frac{p}{100}\right)a = \left(1 - \frac{p^2}{100^2}\right)a = \left(\frac{10000 - p^2}{10000}\right)a$$

- Consider the amounts 'lost' (£1 for A and B above, and 25 pence for C). What possible starting amounts and percentage increases and decreases (possibly different) would lead to a loss of 50 pence or £1? *This means that*

$$a - \left(1 + \frac{p}{100}\right)\left(1 - \frac{p}{100}\right)a = l \text{ or } \frac{ap^2}{10000} = l,$$

  so suitable values for losing 50 pence would be £50 with a 10% increase and 10% decrease or £5000 with a 1% increase and a 1% decrease, etc.

- What other flow diagrams can you make that lead to interesting comparisons? For example, how do two 5% increases compare to a 10% increase? *The answer is that 1.05 × 1.05 = 1.1025, a 10.25% increase, so slightly more than a 10% increase. This happens because the second 5% increase is 5% of a larger quantity than the original starting amount. This is why it makes a difference whether banks add on interest daily, monthly or annually.*

Possible Homework

Learners could photograph products (in a shop or at home) – or find labels on the internet – and 'bleep out' certain parts to create percentage problems; e.g.,

These could form an interesting display.

Patterns

A table such as the one on the next page (available at www.50maths.com) can be a useful *aide-mémoire*, and discussions along the lines of 'What patterns do you see? Can you explain them?' can be useful.

Multipliers and What They Do

multiplier		what it does
0.00	100%	decrease (all gone!)
0.05	95%	decrease
0.10	90%	decrease
0.15	85%	decrease
0.20	80%	decrease
0.25	75%	decrease
0.30	70%	decrease
0.35	65%	decrease
0.40	60%	decrease
0.45	55%	decrease
0.50	50%	decrease
0.55	45%	decrease
0.60	40%	decrease
0.65	35%	decrease
0.70	30%	decrease
0.75	25%	decrease
0.80	20%	decrease
0.85	15%	decrease
0.90	10%	decrease
0.95	5%	decrease
1.00		stays the same (no change!)
1.05	5%	increase
1.10	10%	increase
1.15	15%	increase
1.20	20%	increase
1.25	25%	increase
1.30	30%	increase
1.35	35%	increase
1.40	40%	increase
1.45	45%	increase
1.50	50%	increase
1.55	55%	increase
1.60	60%	increase
1.65	65%	increase
1.70	70%	increase
1.75	75%	increase
1.80	80%	increase
1.85	85%	increase
1.90	90%	increase
1.95	95%	increase
2.00	100%	increase (doubles it!)
2.05	105%	increase

(Obviously the in-between values work in the same way.)

34 Optical Illusions 1

Related Topics

- constructions
- length and angles
- measurement
- proof

Materials Needed

- geometry equipment or dynamic geometry software (or other software)

Appearances can be deceptive. Sometimes you need instruments to measure lengths and angles accurately – first impressions are not always right. Other times you can use reasoning to decide that something is the case even if it doesn't appear to be. Optical illusions can provide a motivation for learners to carry out careful accurate measurement and reasoning on shapes. (In more ordinary situations, learners may see this as pointless, as they are merely confirming what is 'obvious', or at least 'unremarkable'.) The act of constructing these for oneself leads to seeing the illusion aspect appear before your eyes. There is a strong incentive for learners to be careful and accurate in what they do and for rigorous checking by peers.

1 The *Müller-Lyer Illusion* is quite well known, though nonetheless eye-rubbingly deceptive:

(The two horizontal lines are actually the same length.)

2 *Ponzo's Illusion*: Which horizontal line is longer?

Which of these two versions is the more convincing? Why?

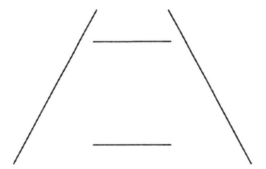 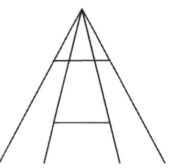

3 *T-Illusion*: Which line is longer, the vertical or the horizontal?

4   *Angle Arms Illusion*: Which angle is larger?

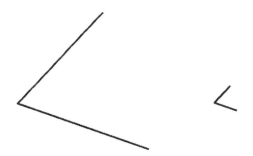

5   *Parallelogram Illusion*: Which of the two dashed lines is longer?

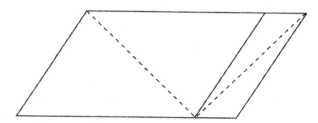

Make an accurate copy of this drawing with a different-shaped parallelogram. (This takes some thought.) In the diagram, the dashed lines make a right angle. Is this possible/necessary in other parallelograms? What shape of parallelogram makes for the most convincing illusion? (A rectangle is obviously no good.)

This is a good task for compass-and-straight-edge constructions, and involves learners in some careful thinking about isosceles triangles.

Learners can get very excited about these illusions and argue about them for a long time. They are also inclined to be very accurate, since peers will 'peer' very closely and be quite harsh about minor imprecision!

If you are uneasy about asking 'trick' questions, such as 'Which line is longer?' when they are the same length, you can ask learners, for example, to 'Compare the lengths of the lines'.

Extension

Learners might like to invent and draw their own ones, either by hand or using computer software such as *Logo,* dynamic geometry software or the drawing tools in a word-processing package. This can make for an absorbing wall display.

Web

These sorts of diagrams appear all over the web and are easy to find if you enter the names given here. A good general source is the 'funny pictures' section of www.keepmeamused. com. Go to www.50maths. com for copies of the ones presented here.

Further Ideas

Other drawings that are rewarding to construct for their own intrinsic illusion value are the *Necker cubes* and the *Penrose triangle.*

35 Optical Illusions 2

Related Topics
- constructions
- measurement
- proof

Materials Needed
- geometry equipment or dynamic geometry software (or other software)

Just because angles *look* the same as each other or lines *appear* parallel in a maths problem, it is unwise to assume that they are. It is all very well the teacher saying this from time to time, but unless learners encounter situations in which the *impression* a diagram makes on their eyes leads them astray, they are unlikely to be particularly cautious. Optical illusions can help learners to trust more in measurement and reasoning than in instant appearances.

A very good task with these illusions is to make copies of them on plain paper. This requires/develops good compass-and-straight-edge skills, and often learners will believe that lines are parallel, etc, only if they actually make them so themselves (usually beginning with that critical feature). Seeing the drawing take shape gradually is a different experience from being confronted all at once by the finished article. At what point do the lines start to look as though they bend? As you talk to learners while they work, you can ask 'Are they still parallel/the same length/etc? Are you sure?'

1 *Café Wall Illusion (or Münsterberg Illusion)*: Are the 'horizontal' lines parallel?

2 *Hering Illusion*: Are the 'horizontal' lines parallel?

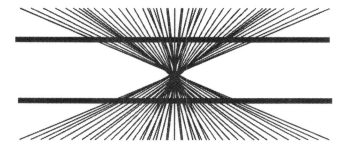

3 *Zöllner's Illusion*: Are the 'vertical' lines parallel?

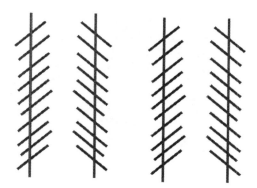

4 *Poggendorff Illusion*: Are the two thinner lines in line with each other or not?

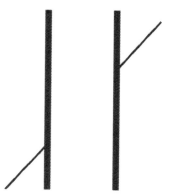

5 *Ehrenstein Illusion*: Is this a square?

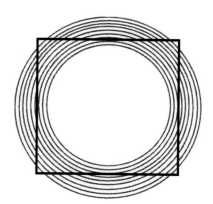

Web

These sorts of diagrams appear all over the web and are easy to find if you enter the names given here. A good general source is the 'funny pictures' section of www.keepmeamused. com. Go to www.50maths. com for copies of the ones presented here.

Further Ideas

Other drawings that are rewarding to construct for their own intrinsic illusion value are the *Necker cubes* and the *Penrose triangle*.

6 *Orbison's Illusion*: Is this a square?

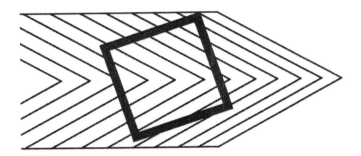

7 *Jastrow Illusion*: Which of these shapes has the greater area?

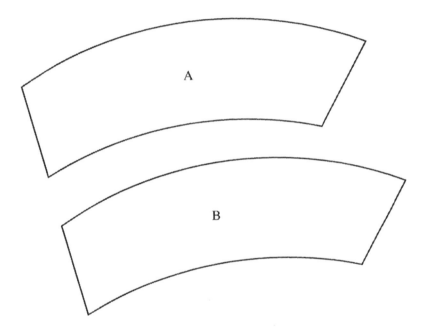

Learners can be very inventive when it comes to designing their own illusions, and even if they are not all completely convincing, a sense is gained of when human perceptions can be trusted and when they ought to be questioned. The value of a lesson like this can go beyond its immediate application to lengths and angles to a more general greater awareness of the need not to make knee-jerk responses to what you are presented with. This will be useful beyond mathematics itself.

Pieces Of Chocolate

36

A number of related tasks are possible on a chocolate bar theme:

Related Topics
- factors
- fractions
- proof
- square numbers

Materials Needed
- some chocolate bars (possibly)

- **How many straight breaks does it take to split a bar of chocolate into all of its pieces? What is the minimum number? What is the maximum number? What other questions can you ask?**

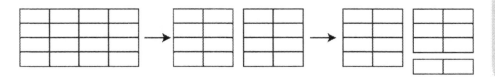

two breaks; three pieces so far

Each break produces one more piece, so for n pieces you will need $n - 1$ breaks, no matter how you do it. This can be a surprising outcome, especially as it does not depend on the positions of the breaks.

- **What if you break up the bar while it is still wrapped up?** *You don't need so many straight line breaks now, since the wrapper holds the broken pieces together for the next break. For an $x \times y$ bar, the total number of breaks is $x + y - 2$, so it depends on the shape of the bar, not just the total number of pieces.*

- **How many possible** ▭▭ **-shaped pieces can be made from a rectangular bar of chocolate?** *In the above-shaped bar, there are three possibilities in each row, so $4 \times 3 = 12$ altogether, or $y(x - 1)$ in general, for an $x \times y$ bar.*

- **You could call the above piece a 2×1 shaped piece. How many possible $a \times b$ shaped pieces are there in an $x \times y$ bar of chocolate?** *The answer is $(x - a + 1)(y - b + 1)$, provided that $a < x$ and $b < y$. (Otherwise there are none, of course, because the bar is too small.)*

- **How many possible rectangles of *any* size can you get out of the *top* row?** *You can get 1×1 (four), 2×1 (three), 3×1 (two), 4×1 (one), which makes 10 altogether. In general, with n pieces, there will be*

$$^{n+1}C_2 = \frac{n(n+1)}{2}$$

since you can imagine 10 vertical positions, any two of which define a rectangle. This can be a way into triangle numbers.

- **How many possible rectangles of *any* size can you get out of the *whole bar*?** *The answer, by similar reasoning, is*

$$^{x+1}C_2 \, {}^{y+1}C_2 = \frac{xy(x+1)(y+1)}{4}$$

(This is sometimes known as the 'How many rectangles are there on a chessboard?' problem.)

- If you think about the top row only – ▢▢▢▢ – how many possible ways are there of splitting this up into pieces of chocolate? *Depending how you count them, there are eight: 4 (leave it alone), 3 + 1, 1 + 3, 2 + 2, 2 + 1 + 1, 1 + 2 + 1, 1 + 1 + 2, 1 + 1 + 1. In general, you can compose n rectangles (what we are doing here) in 2^{n-1} ways, because there are $(n - 1)$ joins between pieces of chocolate, each of which can be either intact or broken (2 ways). If the order doesn't matter (so that, for example, 2 + 1 + 1, 1 + 2 + 1 and 1 + 1 + 2 are all counted as the same), the process is called* partitioning *and the answer comes to 5. The partitions for 1, 2, 3, 4, … pieces are the* partition numbers: *1, 2, 3, 5, 7, 11, 15, 22, 30, 42, 56, …*

- How many ways are there of splitting the whole bar into pieces of any size? *The answer to this is very dependent on the exact rules about what you are allowed to do and how you count the pieces.*

- How many different 2×3 rectangles, say, are there in the chocolate bar? *If we count 2×3 as being the same as 3×2 (i.e., the pieces of chocolate are square), then there are 12. In general, there will be $(y - b + 1)(x - a + 1) + (x - b + 1)(y - a + 1)$ different rectangles of shape $a \times b$ in an $x \times y$ chocolate bar, assuming that $a \ne b$.*

Questions that may arise when working on this task include: Is a square a rectangle? Is a 'one-by-something' rectangle a 'proper' rectangle?

Contexts such as these can be excellent for inviting learners to pose their own questions. It is possible to build a lesson around an 'object', such as a pencil or a football, by asking 'What maths is there in this?', and learners can be very creative. There is a similar richness about tasks based on drawing straight lines on a piece of paper and counting the maximum possible number of crossing points, the number of bounded regions, the number of exterior regions and the number of triangles.

Playing At Transformations

37

There are various transformations board games in common circulation, but, as with many educational games, the biggest benefit may come from *designing* the game rather than *playing* it. With that in mind, it is possible to ask learners in groups to devise games that will involve the players in working on the topic of transformations. (Pupils could be asked to try to make transformations *visually* part of the game, rather than merely producing cards with questions like 'If you reflect the point (4, −7) in the *x*-axis, where will the image be?' and just moving one square round a board if you get it right.)

An example is below:

The 'Two-Four' board game is a game for two players. (You need two dice for each game, but no counters.)

Throw two normal dice. Interpret the scores as coordinates either way round; e.g., if you get 3 and 5 you can take it as (3, 5) or (5, 3). This is your starting position.

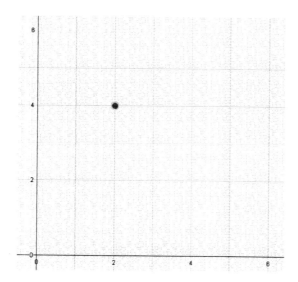

Now you have to get to the *magic point (2, 4)*, marked with a dot (the magic point is always the same), by *one single transformation*, which you have to state fully.

Related Topic
- transformations

Materials Needed
- dice
- glue and sticky tape
- paper of various colours and sizes
- pens
- scissors

Your options are:

- any reflection (state the mirror line)
- any rotation (state the angle, sense and centre of rotation)
- a translation of *1 unit (only)* horizontally *or* vertically (not both)

So from (3, 5) I could rotate 90° anticlockwise about (3, 4), for instance.

If you do it right, you get a point. If you miss the spot, you get nothing and it is the other person's go.

If you are lucky enough to throw a 2 and a 4, then you win straight away on that go and it is the other person's turn.

Whoever has the bigger score after 12 goes is the winner.

Notice here the limitations on translation that are put in place to prevent the game from being too easy.

Depending on how much time you are going to allocate to this, you need to decide how long the groups will have to design and make their game. (The danger is that this over-runs and you end up with very little time to play them!)

Extensions

Making up puzzles relating to transformations can be a useful task and involve some difficult logical thinking. Here is an example:

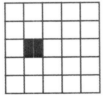

By shading *exactly 3 more squares* each time, can you produce a finished diagram with exactly

1   1 line of symmetry?

2   2 lines of symmetry?

3   4 lines of symmetry?

© Alana Chen, Year 7

Possible answers are shown below:

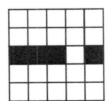 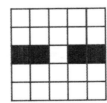 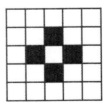

Restrictions on the order of rotational symmetry can also be included, and constructing puzzles which have *one and only one* solution can be challenging!

Round The Back

38

This does take a little preparation, but then you can use it with all your classes, whatever age. I have found Year 7 to be often much better than Year 13 – and maths teachers are among the worst!

Photocopy two copies of the design below (available at www.50maths.com) onto different coloured pieces of card. Cut them out and glue them back-to-back so that *if* you could see through the card (which you *mustn't* be able to) the one on the back would be 60° (two divisions) *anticlockwise* further round than the one on the front. (This will work whichever side you count as 'front' or 'back'.) Then laminate it.

> The dashed arrow in the diagram shows the position of the arrow on the back as it *would* be seen if you could see through the card, which of course you can't.

Related Topic
• symmetry

Material Needed
• the arrow card (described below)

Web
A template for the arrow card is available at www.50maths.com.

Hold the card with your fingers at the 9 o'clock and 3 o'clock points and with the blue side (say) showing the arrow pointing to 4 o'clock, as in the picture above. Then say, 'When the arrow on the *blue* side is pointing to 4 o'clock … [rotate the card about the diameter joining 3 o'clock to 9 o'clock] … the *yellow* side has the arrow *also* pointing to 4 o'clock.' Spin it back to how it was at the start. Then *rotate* the card so that the blue side has the arrow pointing to, say, 6 o'clock. 'When the *blue* side has the arrow pointing to *6* o'clock … [make as if you're going to rotate about the *new* 3 o'clock to 9 o'clock diameter, but don't actually do it] … which way will the arrow on the *yellow* side be pointing?' *The answer is 2 o'clock.*

There are lots of similar questions you can ask; e.g., 'With this rotation, what other time(s) will be the same on both sides?', but it can be better at this point to do nothing else apart from repeat what you've done exactly and then hide the card away and ask learners to discuss in small groups. They might attempt to reproduce the card themselves (even this is not necessarily that easy) and come up with conjectures about the connections between the two sides.

In general, '*n*' o'clock on one side corresponds to '8 − *n*' o'clock on the other if *n* is between 1 and 7. Otherwise, '*n*' o'clock corresponds to '20 − *n*' o'clock. (In all cases it is '20 − n (mod 12)'.) The 4 o'clock to 10 o'clock diameter is a line of symmetry.

Extensions

- What if the original card is made differently, so that the relationship between the arrows on both sides is different? Can you generalize what would happen then?
- Or if you rotated about a different line? There are endless possibilities for extending this puzzle, and the thinking involves quite a hard combination of rotation and reflection.
- If you look at yourself in a mirror, your left and right sides are swapped over but your head and feet are the same way round. Why is this? What happens if you look in a mirror while lying on the floor? How does the mirror 'know' which way is horizontal and which way is vertical? What would happen if you were in zero gravity orbiting around the earth and looked in a mirror?

Shapeshifters

39

Begin with a fairly simple shape, such as the polygon *ABCDE* below, and repeatedly translate it by an amount $\left(\begin{smallmatrix}4\\1\end{smallmatrix}\right)$ in this case) so that each resulting image lies adjacent to the previous shape:

Related Topics
• arithmetic sequences
• coordinates
• translation

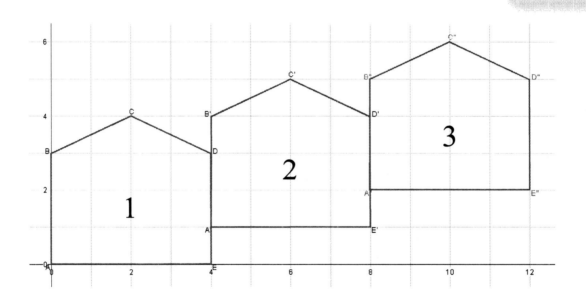

Construct a table as follows:

vertex	shape 1	shape 2	shape 3	shape ...	shape n
A	(0, 0)	(4, 1)	(8, 2)	...	$(4n-4, n-1)$
B	(0, 3)	(4, 4)	(8, 5)	...	$(4n-4, n+2)$
C	(2, 4)	(6, 5)	(10, 6)	...	$(4n-2, n+3)$
D	(4, 3)	(8, 4)	(12, 5)	...	$(4n, n+2)$
E	(4, 0)	(8, 1)	(12, 2)	...	$(4n, n-1)$

Clearly the last column will be the trickiest to complete, generalizing the positions of the vertices of the nth shape. Considering the 10th or 100th shape may help to ascertain where the nth would be. Since the motion is stated to be a fixed translation, learners do not have to assume without justification that obvious numerical patterns will continue in obvious ways – a common problem with sequence tasks. The visual movement of the constant translation becomes a model for a linear sequence because it is apparent from the translation operation that points will move fixed distances in fixed directions.

Learners can select their own choice of translation on a new shape. Translation vectors can include negative numbers, resulting in patterns that cascade downwards or leftwards or both. Coordinates may be fractions.

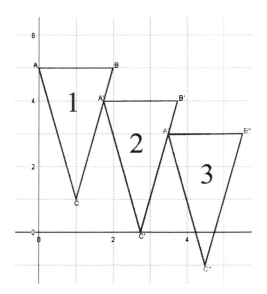

A full generalization might be the statement that under n operations of the translation $\begin{pmatrix} a \\ b \end{pmatrix}$, the point (x, y) moves to the point $(x + a(n-1), y + b(n-1))$.

Extensions

- Choose a translation for a given shape (or a shape for a given translation) such that a specified shape number (e.g., the 100th) will have a specified vertex (e.g., the top of the roof of our 'house' shape) at a specified point (e.g. (50, 50)). For example, How many possible translation vectors (containing integers only) will take our house shape to a place where the point at the top of our roof is (50, 50)? *From (2, 4) to (50, 50) is the vector $\begin{pmatrix} 46 \\ 48 \end{pmatrix}$, so any integer vectors of which an integer scalar multiple equals this will do; i.e., $\begin{pmatrix} 23 \\ 24 \end{pmatrix}$ and $\begin{pmatrix} 46 \\ 48 \end{pmatrix}$ are the only possible answers.*

- Imagine stacking plastic cups. Estimate how high one plastic cup is. How high are two plastic cups when stacked? How high are 20 plastic cups?
  Typical answers might be 9 cm for one, say, but 9.5 cm for two; nth term = ½n + 8½, so 20th term = 18.5 cm.

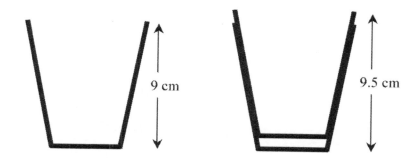

- A possible idea for sequences lessons is *serial sevens*: counting down from 100 in sevens. It is used as a clinical test to help assess patients after possible head injury and is also sometimes used to test for impairment by drugs/alcohol, so it might be worth practising!
- Using a spreadsheet, ask learners to pick two starting numbers and enter these into the first two cells in a column. Select these cells and drag down from the bottom right corner of the lower cell. This generates more terms of the arithmetic sequence beginning with these two terms. The task can be to predict later terms or to find a formula for the nth term that will produce a matching column of numbers alongside this one.

40

Sticky Polygons

Related Topics
- inequalities
- number bonds
- polygons

Materials Needed
- compasses (perhaps)
- Cuisenaire rods (or linking cubes) or straws and scissors
- rulers

Web
For a spreadsheet of results, go to www.50maths.com.

- You have a set of sticks of various lengths (e.g., integer lengths from 1 to 6). Take three sticks – can you make a triangle with them? When? Why?

Many pupils will think that you will always be able to, no matter what the lengths of the sticks, but that is not true. Learners will come across impossible examples and can be encouraged to construct rules about when a triangle will exist and when it won't.

- If there is just *one* stick of each length (1 to 6) available, then there will be $^6C_3 = 20$ possible sets of three sticks. How many of these will make a triangle? *The answer is 7 of them, but another 6 of them 'just' fail to make a triangle; i.e., make a straight line. With different ranges of sticks, the following numbers of triangles are obtained:*

sticks available (one of each)	number of (non-zero-area) triangles possible
1–3	0
1–4	1
1–5	3
1–6	7
1–7	13
1–8	22

The answer is that each side in the triangle must be shorter than the *sum* of the other two but longer than the *difference* between the other two. So if the sides are of length *a*, *b* and *c*, then $a < b + c$ and $a > | b - c |$ (with similar inequalities with the letters in the other permutations) – the *Triangle Inequality*.

Learners may find it easier to see why this is so if they try to construct some 'impossible triangles' (such as 3 cm, 5 cm, 10 cm) with ruler and compasses.

- What if you take four/five/six/seven sticks? Can you make a quadrilateral? Can you make a rectangle?

With four sticks, to make a triangle you obviously need to pair two of them (there are three ways of doing that, provided all the sticks are of different lengths) and then see whether the combined length, with the lengths of the other two sticks, will make a triangle. Whether you can make a rectangle with four sticks is pretty obvious (there must be two equal-length pairs), but with five or more sticks it is less straightforward. Puzzles such as the following are easy to make up, by starting with the complete rectangle and breaking it down, but can be quite difficult to solve. There can be a lot of potential in learners devising problems for one another.

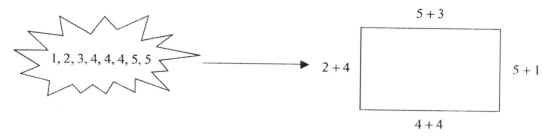

- When can you make more than one rectangle?
- When can you make a square?
- When can you make other polygons?

Striking Angles

Making their own posters can be a good way for learners to collect, consolidate and reinforce facts which it may be considered important for them to remember.

1 Straight Lines

Learners can be invited to make posters to illustrate ideas to do with angles in a striking eye-catching way. Drawings could be based around key words, as in the example below:

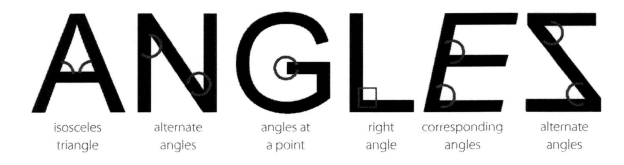

| isosceles triangle | alternate angles | angles at a point | right angle | corresponding angles | alternate angles |

Looking for something unusual or funny may make an idea more memorable; e.g.,

© Sabrina Gillespie, Year 8

2   Circles

Circular filter papers are not expensive, and it is difficult to cut out an accurate circle by hand. Learners can find the centre by folding two diameters and locating the crossing point. With the centre marked, draw a chord 3 cm (say) long and cut off the minor segment produced:

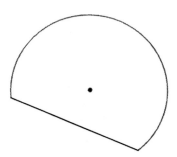

Then cut out or fold any concave quadrilateral (not necessarily symmetrical) with one vertex at the centre and another on the circumference, such as the one below:

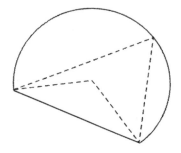

Although different learners' quadrilaterals will be different, because the chord is the same the angles at the centre and the circumference will be the same for each person (and the angle at the centre will be twice the angle at the circumference), so different people's shapes will fit together in this way:

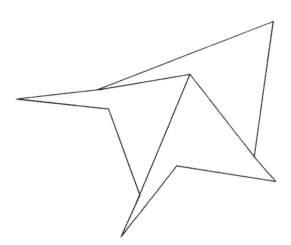

This can contribute to a memorable poster on 'circle theorems'.

Materials Needed

- circular filter papers (ask a technician from the science department)
- geometry equipment
- large paper
- long rulers
- pens
- scrap paper triangles of various shapes and sizes

Demonstrating Properties

- A filter paper can be folded in half and then two more folds from the ends of the diameter can produce a right-angled triangle in a semicircle (*Thales' Theorem*). (These right-angled pieces could go in the four corners of a poster on circle theorems.)
- Guillotine 'random' triangles from odd bits of scrap paper (this is quick and easy) and give one to each learner. 'Hold up your triangle if it's right-angled/ obtuse-angled/isosceles, etc.' This establishes that there is a wide variety of shapes and sizes.
  - Learners then fold the angle bisectors of each vertex by folding pairs of edges together. The fold lines produced meet at the *incentre*, and a circle centred on this point (the *incircle*) is the *inscribed circle* of the triangle (the largest circle that will fit inside it).
  - Start again with a new triangle and fold *perpendicular* bisectors instead, by folding pairs of *vertices* together. The three fold lines will meet inside the triangle only if the triangle is acute-angled. If the triangle is obtuse-angled, they will meet outside, and if the triangle is right-angled they will meet at the mid-point of the hypotenuse (Thales' Theorem again). If you want all learners to be able to locate the *circumcentre* (the centre of the *circumcircle*), the same approach can be used, but triangles other than acute-angled ones will need to be *drawn* on larger pieces of paper.

Switching Switches

42

A '5 by 3' grid of lights is installed in the ceiling with a corresponding '5 by 3' grid of light switches on the wall. All the wiring is correct, but unfortunately the electrician screws the switches panel upside down. Which light will the switch 4 along and 2 up – i.e., (4, 2) – operate? *The answer is light (2, 2).* **Generalize.**

Related Topic

• rotational symmetry

It is sensible to draw diagrams and look at specific cases to get a sense of what is going on. An alternative context might be the more common scenario, perhaps, of reaching a lighting panel from the 'wrong side' of the lighting desk and having to turn around mentally to get the right switch for the light you want.

This can be a good problem for learners to work on, because the algebra, though complicated in detail, does not involve anything more than addition and subtraction, and so generalization from numerical examples and an awareness of the structure of the situation is accessible.

The answer is that in an 'a by b' array of lights, switch (x, y) will operate light $(a - x + 1, b - y + 1)$. (Obviously, 'on' and 'off' would be the wrong way round, also.) The situation is completely symmetrical, so, alternatively, light (x, y) will be controlled by switch $(a - x + 1, b - y + 1)$. This is an example of *self-inverse functions* – if you replace x by $(a - x + 1)$ and y by $(b - y + 1)$ in the expressions above, you obtain x and y respectively.

Extensions

- What if the light switches were installed *sideways* instead?

There are two possibilities for 'sideways': a 90° *anticlockwise* rotation of the switches means that switch (x, y) will operate light $(y, b - x + 1)$ whereas a 90° *clockwise* rotation of the switches means that switch (x, y) will operate light $(a - y + 1, x)$.

This time, if you start with the position of the light that you want to activate and you want to know which switch controls it (probably a more realistic situation), the result is different expressions. Instead, you need the result for the *opposite* rotation (i.e., reverse the two statements above).

- If you had circular light switches (of the 'push-on-push-off' variety, say) and a circular layout of lights in the room, then there would be many more possible installation confusions; e.g., the diagram below:

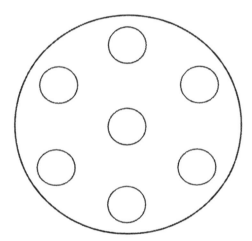

In this case there are five possible incorrect angles at which the panel can be installed, and only the middle switch is unambiguous. The first stage with this problem will probably be to adopt a convenient and logical way of numbering the seven switches and lights.

That Wheeling Feeling

43

Modern society is highly dependent on wheels, yet many people find it very hard to visualize the path traced out by a point on a moving wheel, and it can provide an interesting context for locus.

- If you ride a bicycle in a straight line along flat horizontal ground, what path is followed by the valve on one of the wheels? (Or you could imagine a chalk mark or drawing pin or bit of chewing gum on the tyre.)

Learners can experiment with a circular coin on paper. (This is easier in pairs, because one person can rotate the coin and the other person can mark positions on the paper.) *If you assume that the valve (or whatever) is exactly on the circumference of the wheel, the answer is a cycloid:*

Learners often think that there will be loops, but there won't if the point is exactly on the circumference of the wheel and there is no slipping. Watching a rolling object carefully may be convincing.

- What about the locus of a position *part way* along a spoke of the wheel? *A curtate cycloid is produced – the same shape used for the arches in some violins.*

- You can consider positions *sticking out* from the circumference of the wheel if you imagine a point on the flange of a train wheel. You then *do* get little loops in the curve, as these points actually move *backwards* – in the opposite direction to the motion of the train. The curve is called a *prolate cycloid*.

- What about the locus of one of the pedals? What happens when you change gear?
- What about a bicycle with smaller wheels? How would the drawing change?
- What if you pedal faster?

Related Topics
- curves
- locus

Materials Needed
- a bicycle (possibly)
- circular filter papers (various sizes) – ask a technician from the science department
- coins
- compasses
- paper plates and coloured pens

Web
If you search for 'cycloid', there are plenty of sites with moving demos showing the developing locus as the wheel rolls along the ground.

Further Idea
See if anyone has a Spirograph® set they can bring in.

Related questions could include the following:

- What if a circular coin rolls around the circumference of another identical coin? What is the locus of a fixed point on the circumference of the moving coin? *The answer is a cardioid, and note that the moving coin rotates twice in making one circuit round the fixed coin.*

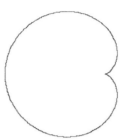

- What if the fixed coin is smaller/larger than the moving coin? *You get an epicycloid, of which the cardioid is just the simplest example.*
- What if a circle rolls around the *inside* of a larger circle? *In that case you get a hypocycloid, such as a deltoid or an astroid.*

Extensions

- Take a circular filter paper and mark a dot anywhere in the interior except the centre. Fold in a point on the edge so that it exactly meets the dot. Unfold and repeat for a different adjacent edge point. Keep going using edge points all the way round the circle. What shape is 'enveloped' by the fold lines? How does it depend on the position of the dot you originally drew? *The answer is that you get an ellipse with its two foci at the centre of the circle and at the dot you originally drew.*
- Try the same thing with a rectangle but just fold points on the edge of *one* side onto the dot in the interior. *This time you should get a parabola, with its focus at the point you originally drew.*
- To fold a *hyperbola* (one branch of it), you need to *draw* a circle on a piece of paper and mark a point somewhere *outside* the circle, and then repeatedly fold various points on the edge of the circle onto this point. (The easiest way is to draw a circle on an ordinary rectangular piece of paper, mark one of the corners of the paper as the fixed point and repeatedly fold this corner in to the circle.)

The Bear's Ring

44

One way of practising using bearings without needing any textbooks or photocopied diagrams is to use coordinates. This provides an opportunity for an interesting investigation, possibly involving some trigonometry, algebra and inequalities, depending on what learners already know or are comfortable working with.

- Taking the y-axis as North, what is the bearing of $(3, 4)$ from $(0, 0)$? *The answer is 36.9°.*
- What is the bearing of $(0, 0)$ from $(3, 4)$? *The answer is 216.9°.*
- More generally, what is the bearing of (a, b) from $(0, 0)$?
- What is the bearing of $(0, 0)$ from (a, b)?
- What is the bearing of (c, d) from (a, b), where any of a, b, c and d could be negative?

A possible computer-room task is to construct a spreadsheet that gives the bearing when you enter the coordinates. (Go to www.50maths.com for mine.)

For learners who have not met sin, cos and tan, this is a task involving accurate measuring of angles and looking for relationships between the bearing and the back-bearing. Learners may notice that a translation of both points by the same vector does not change the bearings. They may be able to express algebraically when the bearing will be 000°, 045°, 090°, etc. They might be able to prove a relationship between a bearing and a back-bearing.

The relationship of a bearing to the back-bearing is as follows:

If the bearing of A from B is θ, then the bearing of B from A is
$\theta + 180$ if $0 \leq \theta < 180$
$\theta - 180$ if $0 \leq \theta < 360$.
Or you can just say that bearing $= (\theta + 180) \bmod 360$ in all cases.

For learners with some trigonometry, a fuller solution might be possible. It is helpful to think separately about four quadrants centred on (a, b). The signs of $(b - d)$ and $(c - a)$ will be different depending on where (c, d) is in relation to (a, b) (see below).

The two left-hand formulae (where $c < a$) are equivalent to each other (since $\tan^{-1}(-x) = -\tan^{-1}x$), as are the two right-hand formulae (where $c > a$). The case

---

Related Topic
- bearings

Materials Needed
- protractors
- squared paper

Web
For a spreadsheet that gives you the bearing when you enter the two pairs of coordinates, go to www.50maths.com. This can be useful for marking and for plenary discussions.

Further Idea
Learners might like to find out about polar coordinates.

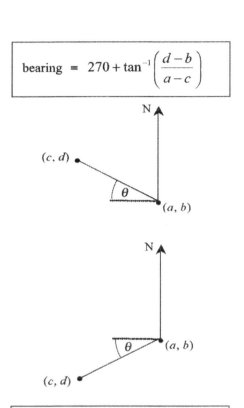

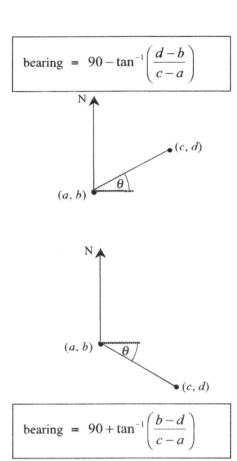

$$\text{bearing} = 270 + \tan^{-1}\left(\frac{d-b}{a-c}\right)$$

$$\text{bearing} = 90 - \tan^{-1}\left(\frac{d-b}{c-a}\right)$$

$$\text{bearing} = 270 - \tan^{-1}\left(\frac{b-d}{a-c}\right)$$

$$\text{bearing} = 90 + \tan^{-1}\left(\frac{b-d}{c-a}\right)$$

where $a = c$ needs separate treatment. So one way of expressing the overall result is:

The bearing of (c, d) from (a, b) is given by:

$$270 + \tan^{-1}\left(\frac{b-d}{c-a}\right) \text{ if } a > c$$

$$90 + \tan^{-1}\left(\frac{b-d}{c-a}\right) \text{ if } a < c$$

000° if $a = c$ and $b < d$
180° if $a = c$ and $b > d$

A lot of good thinking is achieved even if all the details of this solution are not obtained. At the very least, learners are less likely to think that a bearing from A to B is the same thing as a bearing from B to A.

Extension

A *bear* buries a *ring* at a particular pair of coordinates. Give instructions from the origin for a roundabout route to get there: 'Go this far on this bearing and then this far on this bearing', etc. See if someone else can draw it out and find the coordinates where the ring is buried.

The Time Is 'Right'

45

Imagine an analogue clock. (It might be useful to have one handy, or at least a picture of one, although you may wish to encourage mental visualization.) When are the hour and minute hands at *right angles* to each other?

If pupils offer 3:00 or 9:00, just say 'Yes' and ask for more answers. If they offer times that are *approximately* right, such as 12:15, you could say 'Yeeeeees', with a grudging tone. Either someone will comment on what you are doing or you can draw attention to it: 'Why did I say "Yes" to Mandeep but "Yeeeees" to Ben?'

Alternatively, you could ask learners to write possible times on mini-whiteboards and then sort them into three groups: 'Amy stand on that side; Saboor stand in the middle', etc, depending on whether their answer is exactly 90° or slightly less or slightly more. (Pupils who realize the rule can be encouraged to assist in the sorting rather than reveal the rule.)

Some times are a little bit less than 90°; e.g., 10:05, 11:10, 12:15, 1:20, 2:25, etc.

Some times are a little bit more than 90°; e.g., 4:05, 5:10, 6:15, 7:20, 8:25, etc.

You could create two lists on the board and ask pupils to suggest additions to each. Justifying which list their time belongs to can be a useful discussion task.

Then ask learners, perhaps in pairs, to decide what the angle is between the hands at a particular time such as 9:30 or 10:00. (You could see what convenient time it is close to at that moment in the lesson, perhaps.) It may be helpful to remind pupils that 'all the way round is 360°', but you shouldn't need to give much more assistance than that at the start.

Extensions

- When you reflect an angle in a mirror, it stays the same. What time do you get when you reflect 3:30? *So 3:30 and 8:30 are both 75° – this saves some of the work.*
- If this is the angle, what could the time be? Are there any angles (< 360°) that the hands *never* make with each other at *any* time? *No, providing the hands move smoothly.*

Related Topic
- angle sum at a point

Materials Needed
- an actual clock (possibly) or a picture/model of one
- calculators
- protractors

Web
For a spreadsheet that works out the angle when you type in the time, go to www.50maths.com. (This can be useful for marking work or for using during plenaries.) There is also a page of blank clock faces.

Further Idea
Make a 'broken plate' puzzle which has exactly 1, 2 or 3 solutions. (Two identical plain circular plates have fallen onto the floor and broken into pieces along their diameters. In how many ways can you fit them back together?)

- If you could tell from the daylight *roughly* what time it was and all you could ask someone was 'What angle is it?', would that be enough to get you the exact time?
- How many times between 12:00 midday and 12:00 midnight are the hands at right angles? *The answer is 22. It is 3:00 and 9:00 which stop the answer from being 24.*
- When do the hands point in exactly the *same* direction? *12:00 (obviously), then every 1¹⁄₁₁ hours after that. This is because it happens 11 times in 12 hours, and at regular intervals, so you need to do 12 ÷ 11 to find out their frequency.*
- How many times do the hands make 180°, like they do at 6:00? *Again, it's only 11 times, not 12. When you're counting, watch out that you don't double count around 12:30. So it is also every 1¹⁄₁₁ hours after 6:00.*
- Make a formula (or a spreadsheet – for mine go to www.50maths.com) which calculates the angle given the time.

Dizzy

Younger pupils might like to take to the floor and demonstrate an angle by turning round that amount. Angles more than 360° are the most interesting. For example, what does a 1000° turn look like? *Just over 2¾ turns – don't get dizzy!* 'Guesstimate my angle!' 'How many degrees makes me dizzy?' This can provide some light relief at those moments when learners have been sitting still for too long.

Three Squares And A Triangle

46

Pick any two of these four shapes:

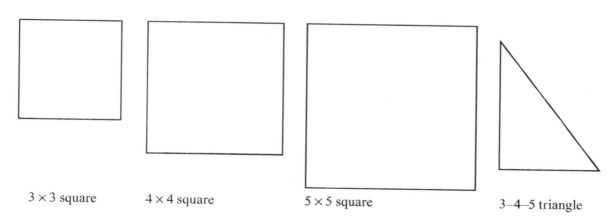

3 × 3 square   4 × 4 square   5 × 5 square   3—4—5 triangle

Place them alongside each other (or overlapping), and work out the area and perimeter of the combined shape. Plot the results as the coordinates (area, perimeter) on a scattergraph:

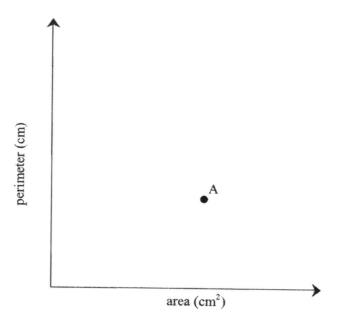

(You can either label the shapes 'A', 'B', etc or perhaps do a small sketch of each one in the right place on the graph. An alternative is to do a *giant* scattergraph on the wall and have learners Blu Tack® their shapes onto the graph in the correct positions.)

Related Topics
- area and perimeter
- ratio
- similar shapes

Overlapping squares need careful counting/measuring to get the correct perimeter; e.g.,

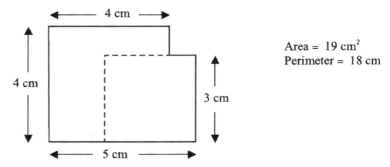

Area = 19 cm^2
Perimeter = 18 cm

Overlapping a triangle and a square needs application of ratio in similar triangles (neither trigonometry itself nor Pythagoras' Theorem are needed); e.g.,

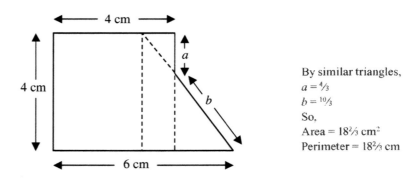

By similar triangles,
$a = \frac{4}{3}$
$b = \frac{10}{3}$
So,
Area = $18\frac{2}{3}$ cm^2
Perimeter = $18\frac{2}{3}$ cm

Learners can be encouraged to give exact answers as fractions but to check that they are in the right range by converting to decimals and measuring their diagrams.

- Try to find shapes where the area and the perimeter are numerically equal (as in the situation above).
- Try to find shapes that lead to positions on the graph which are currently 'unoccupied territory'.

Extensions

- In theory, any shape can be said to have an equal area and perimeter; it just depends on the units. For example, a learner might invent a unit (call it a 'pen-top', say) equal to 1.25 cm, so that the 5×5 square, measured in those units, has a perimeter of 16 pen-tops and an area of 16 square-pen-tops. Perhaps they could devise some suitable units for some of their other shapes.
- Invite someone else to sort out their shapes (by eye – no measuring or calculating allowed) into three categories: area << perimeter; area ≈ perimeter, area >> perimeter. It's pretty difficult – and disagreements provide a motivation for careful calculation and checking.

Timber!

47

If a straight line falls across a squared grid, how many angles are produced? (For example, a tree falls onto a pavement or, in the classroom, a window pole or metre stick lands on a tiled floor.) You may want to set this up by drawing lines across a squared whiteboard or by offering drinking straws to learners. It can be helpful to have squared paper containing relatively large-sized squares (e.g., 4 cm × 4 cm). A template is available at www.50maths.com.

This is a good problem for logical exhaustive thinking and for 'discovering' (perhaps again) the angle relationships produced by a transversal across two parallel lines. Although it makes no difference, in most cases, whether the grid is 'square' or 'rectangular' as far as the angles are concerned, squared paper is obviously more readily available.

The number of different angles produced (depending on how you count them, and ignoring the 90° angles that are already present on the grid) is:

- 0 if the line falls along an existing line
- 1 (90°) if the line falls parallel to an existing line but not along it
- 2 (45° and 135°) if the line falls as a 45° diagonal (whether or not it passes through grid points)
- 3 impossible
- 4 in all other cases (see below)

Where four angles (x, y, a and b below) are produced, their values are linked by three equations, so only one of the angles is 'independent'; i.e., setting the value of any one of the angles determines all the others.

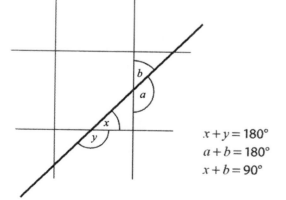

$x + y = 180°$
$a + b = 180°$
$x + b = 90°$

(There are other sets of three equations which can be written, and which can be obtained by eliminating one letter between two of these.)

Related Topics
- angles in triangles
- angles on parallel lines

Materials Needed
- drinking straws (possibly)
- squared paper

Web
For a template of 4 cm × 4 cm squared paper, go to www.50maths.com.

Changing to an *isometric* grid makes the problem more complicated but still utilizes only the same properties of angles in triangles and on parallel lines.

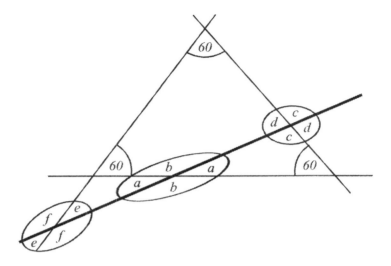

$a + b = 180$

$c + d = 180$

$e + f = 180$

$a + c = 120$

$a + e = 60$

Here we have five dependent variables and one independent.

Relationships

Depending on how pupils are seated, it may be possible to lay a long stick (such as a window pole) across the room so that particular pupils (acting as angles) 'have relationships with each other', such as 'alternate', 'corresponding', 'interior' and 'vertically opposite'. 'Who is alternate to Sofie?'; 'Which people are corresponding to Tanvir?'

Time To Reflect

48

- Imagine a clock with only markings round the edge (no numbers), as shown below. Suppose I take a photograph of the clock at some time and show you the photo. But I *might* have reversed the photograph or I might not. Can you tell? How? Does it depend where the hands are?

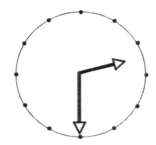

- If I had *rotated* the camera 30° (or any multiple of 30°) before taking the photo, could you tell? How?

You can't tell reflections, because without the numbers (and things like the manufacturer's name, etc) a clock-face has 12 lines of symmetry.

- So if the time is 9:45 on the real clock, what time is it on the reversed (mirror image) clock? *The answer is 2:15.*
- If the time is so many hours (h) and so many minutes (m), what time do you see when you look in the mirror?

Making up algebra for this requires thinking about special cases, such as 'on the hour'. The answer is that the reflected time (hours (h_r) and minutes (m_r)) is given by:

$$
\begin{aligned}
m_r \quad &= 0 && \text{if } m = 0 \\
&= 60 - m && \text{otherwise} \\
h_r \quad &= 12 && \text{if } h = 12 \text{ and } m = 0 \\
&= 12 && \text{if } h = 11 \text{ and } m \neq 0 \\
&= 12 - h && \text{if } h \neq 12 \text{ and } m = 0 \\
&= 11 - h && \text{otherwise}
\end{aligned}
$$

For a spreadsheet which gives the reflected time when you enter the real time (or vice versa, obviously), go to www.50maths.com.

Related Topics
- angles
- reflection symmetry

Materials Needed
A clock or watch without numbers on the face may be useful.

Web
For a spreadsheet which gives the reflected time when you enter the real time (or vice versa, obviously), go to www.50maths.com. There is also a sheet of blank clock-faces.

Extension

- What if we include a seconds hand? How does that affect things?

The seconds hand (which is, in fact, 'the third hand'!) messes everything up, with regard to both reflection and rotation of the clock-face. It breaks the symmetry, so that, provided the photograph was accurate enough, you *could* tell that you had an impossible time when you viewed a reflection or rotation. This is not true for every instant but is true for most times.

This idea comes from a particularly good episode of *Columbo* called 'Negative Reaction' (Season 4, Episode 2, 1974).

Tricky Triangles

49

Don't advertise that this lesson is about gradient – this will kill the activity. Instead, give pupils the diagram on the right – you could hand it out on sheets, but it may be better (as you will see) to keep it at arm's length by drawing it on the board. (If you have a projector with access to the internet, just go to www.50maths.com.)

Ask learners to find the areas of each of the two triangles and of the rectangle, and also to find the area of the whole figure. Don't tell them anything else. Encourage the learners to notice what they're doing, but don't be too helpful!

Learners will find that the areas 'don't add up':

area of large triangle + area of rectangle + area of small triangle $\neq$ area of whole figure

$$\frac{10 \times 7}{2} + 4 \times 7 + \frac{4 \times 3}{2} \quad \neq \quad \frac{14 \times 10}{2} \quad \text{i.e. } 69 \neq 70$$

The purpose of the lesson is for learners to try to make sense of the diagram. They might begin perhaps by making an accurate copy of it on paper.

The problem is that the slopes of the slanting lines are not the same. There is a very-obtuse-angled triangle (shaded in the very exaggerated drawing below) of area 1 cm².

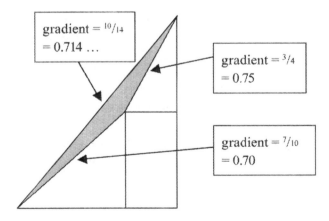

After some time, the learners will appreciate that the angles of these lines are different and begin to express it by talking about how many squares along and

Related Topics
• area
• gradient

Material Needed
• the starting image (on paper or the board), which is available at www.50maths.com.

up the lines go. Drawing this into a whole-class discussion will lead naturally to a formal concept of gradient.

Extension

Learners can make up their own deceptive diagrams. One possibility is a dissection paradox, such as the following fairly well-known one:

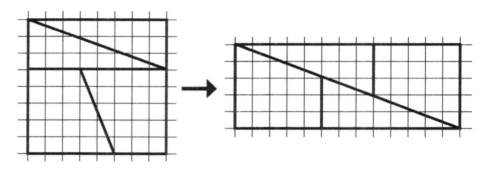

You cut up the left-hand shape ($8 \times 8 = 64$ cm^2) and rearrange the pieces to make the right-hand one ($13 \times 5 = 65$ cm^2).

This one (below) is similar and can be extremely mystifying:

Cut out these pieces:

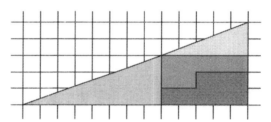

Then rearrange them – and there is a hole!

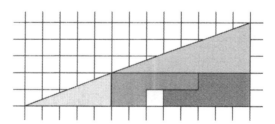

There are links with the *Fibonacci Sequence* (1, 1, 2, 3, 5, 8, 13, …). Because consecutive terms in the sequence have a ratio that converges to the golden ratio (1.61803 …), values such as $^8/_5$ and $^{13}/_8$ are fairly close to each other, and so consecutive terms of the sequence provide good values for the various lengths if you want to produce deceptively similar gradients.

Twenty-Four
Square Centimetres

50

Guillotine some centimetre-squared paper to A5 size and give one sheet to each pair of learners. Each pupil takes it in turn to draw any polygon they like with an area of 24 cm². (24 is a useful number to choose because it has many factors, allowing lots of possible shapes with integer side lengths.) The only rules about the polygons that learners may draw are that all shapes:

- must have a maximum of *six sides*; and
- must not overlap with any shape already drawn on the paper.

The 'six-sides-or-fewer' rule is designed to allow 'L'-shapes but to rule out excessively staircase-like polygons that can make the game too easy. The loser is the first person not to be able to go.

The competitive element encourages rigorous checking of the other person's shape, and the constraints of available space on the paper can push learners into quite complex ideas as the game develops.

You may wish to discuss beforehand good ways of finding the areas of awkward shapes drawn on square grids. Rather than splitting the shapes up into triangles and rectangles, it is often easier to enclose the whole shape in the smallest possible rectangle and then subtract whatever rectangles and triangles are necessary around the edge. For example, see below:

Related Topics
- areas of polygons
- fractions

Material Needed
- squared paper

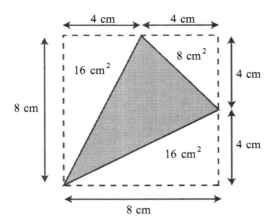

Area of triangle =
$8 \times 8 - 16 - 16 - 8 = 24$ cm²

A common revelation while playing this game is that the diagonal of a unit square is longer than a unit, so that a '2 × 12' tilted rectangle (at 45°), say, would have an area of 48 cm², not 24 cm².

Extensions

- Learners might wish to consider how to adapt/improve the game and have opinions on whether it is better to go first or second.
- An identical game may be played as a whole-class activity on a squared whiteboard, where the number of squares it possesses, and its shape, determine the constraints.
- Learners will be familiar with representing fractions as the shaded or unshaded portions of rectangles (or other shapes) drawn on squared paper. Attempting to draw *'non-obvious shadings'*, however, can be an interesting and beneficial task. For example, the challenge might be to see in how many ways you can shade ⅓, say, of a 3 by 4 rectangle so that it is not immediately apparent that it is ⅓. The idea is that a certain amount of reasoning or counting is necessary to verify it. Learners could construct five or six of these, where all but one are ⅓, and one is only slightly different, the task being to identify the odd one out.
- Another task would be to see which fractions can be displayed on a 3 by 4 rectangle if straight lines between grid points are all that is allowed. There are some examples below:

⅓

¹¹/₂₄

⅓

½

Restrictions can be placed on the number of sides allowed for the shaded shape. Addition of fractions becomes relevant when learners wish to make a fraction slightly larger than one they have already made (e.g., 'How many half squares would I need to add to my ⅓ to make ¾?').

Bibliography

Association of Teachers of Mathematics (1989) *Points of Departure 1–4*, ATM

Banwell, C., Saunders, K. and Tahta, D. (1986) *Starting Points*, Tarquin

Bills, C., Bills, L., Watson, A. and Mason, J. (2004) *Thinkers*, Association of Teachers of Mathematics

Clausen-May, T. (2005) *Teaching Maths to Pupils with Different Learning Styles*, Paul Chapman Publishing

Mason, J. (1999) *Learning and Doing Mathematics*, QED

Ollerton, M. (2002) *Learning and Teaching Mathematics without a Textbook*, Association of Teachers of Mathematics

Ollerton, M. (2005) *100 Ideas for Teaching Mathematics*, Continuum

Ollerton, M. and Watson, A. (2001) *Inclusive Mathematics 11–18*, Continuum

Foster, C. (2003) *Instant Maths Ideas for Key Stage 3 Teachers, Volume 1: Number and Algebra*, Nelson Thornes

Foster, C. (2003) *Instant Maths Ideas for Key Stage 3 Teachers, Volume 2: Shape and Space*, Nelson Thornes

Foster, C. (2003) *Instant Maths Ideas for Key Stage 3 Teachers, Volume 3: Data, Numeracy and ICT*, Nelson Thornes

Foster, C. (2008) *Variety in Mathematics Lessons*, Association of Teachers of Mathematics

There are many other excellent books and resources available from www.atm.org.uk.